DATE DUE

11/21/00			
5/20/01			

What to Do When It Hurts So Bad

What to Do When It Hurts So Bad

Edward Montgomery

Destiny Image Publishers
P.O. Box 310
Shippensburg, PA 17257-0310

"We Publish the Prophets"

ISBN 1-56043-770-7 Casebound
ISBN 1-56043-124-5 Paperback

For Worldwide Distribution
Printed in the U.S.A.

Destiny Image books are available through these fine distributors outside the United States:

Christian Growth, Inc.
Jalan Kilang-Timor, Singapore 0315

Successful Christian Living
Capetown, Rep. of South Africa

Lifestream
Nottingham, England

Vision Resources
Ponsonby, Auckland, New Zealand

Rhema Ministries Trading
Randburg, South Africa

WA Buchanan Company
Geebung, Queensland, Australia

Salvation Book Centre
Petaling, Jaya, Malaysia

Word Alive
Niverville, Manitoba, Canada

This book is dedicated to Saundra. To you, the reader, this name is only one of thousands. But to me it evokes visions of love, patience, encouragement, constructive criticism and the giving of time that belonged to her and my family.

I dedicate this book to Saundra—my wife. Without her this book would only exist in my mind.

Special Thanks

To Jewel, who typed and retyped hundreds of pages of transcript. Thank you, Jewel. To Ron and Veda Shaw, your friendship got us through. To Deborah and Mary, who labored for hours to make sure what I had said was readable. To Pat, my secretary, who started the process. And of course, to the members of Abundant Life Cathedral Church, who had to listen as my ideas developed and redeveloped.

Contents

Foreword

When I was growing up in the church as a young minister, the advice of older ministers was "never get close to your people and never let them know your weaknesses." Even then I wondered if that wouldn't be a lonely way to live. I was seventeen at the time, a "boy preacher," as they called us, I thought it was good advice, it wasn't.

Ed Montgomery draws us into a journey that few ministers ask you to share. He answers the questions most people want to ask, but are afraid of the response. Ed is a gifted communicator with a God-given ability to paint word pictures that capture the ideas with tremendous power. His candor, humor and his very clear focus on the sovereignty of God forces us to face our finite limitations and God's wisdom.

What to Do When It Hurts So Bad is a catharsis, you cannot be a part of the human condition and not find your experience in these pages. And at the same time, you will be supremely encouraged by Pastor Montgomery's insights.

A wise man once said, "Experience is not the best teacher. The best teacher is one who has had an experience and will tell you so you don't have to have the experience." This wonderful book will help you wherever you are in your Christian walk. You will laugh, you will weep, you will marvel at the faithfulness of God, and you will grow. I encourage you to read, *What to Do When It Hurts So Bad* prayerfully, carefully, and expectantly.

Joseph L. Garlington
Senior Pastor
Covenant Church of Pittsburgh

Out of the pain of personal loss, the dark night of deep grief, and the quiet surety of renewed faith, Ed Montgomery has written a book certain to touch readers' hearts.

In the era when the prosperity gospel threatens to undercut the good aspects of the charismatic renewal, Montgomery's book demonstrates the depth of Christian faith held by many charismatics. He demonstrates that the gospel of joy can equip one to face life's tragedies.

Cecile Holmes White
Religion Editor
The Houston Chronicle

Introduction

This book deals with the struggle to find a happy medium between passive religion and spiritual lunacy. I'm a pastor; I preach to hundreds in my congregation and to thousands by way of television each week. Like any speaker, I want to feel that my message is heard and taken into consideration, but I've come to learn that each week's message is heard in the context of weekly problems.

I preach faith on Sunday, yet someone loses it on Monday. On Monday, I encourage families to be strong, yet on Tuesday the divorce papers arrive. When I believe I've given hope for tomorrow, I find out today that someone's business venture went under, a husband has learned his wife has breast cancer, the teenager of a model family has committed suicide, a close family member is on drugs, or a compassionate, giving couple has lost their home.

I wrote this book because it had to be written. The theological shilly-shallying probably will not endear me to my peers, but it is merely a writer's tool designed to provoke thought. My peers will understand, for they are faced daily with the same dilemmas and contradictions as I am.

This book has emerged from the sea of individuals who ache—those nameless faces we see in supermarket lines, traffic jams and elevators. It is targeted to penetrate the theatrical smiles that hide shattered faith, loss of courage and anger aimed at God.

I have tried not to preach to anyone; for this reason I've sprinkled this manuscript with dialogue, satire, humor and honest-to-goodness, real-life illustrations. Every now and then, I'll zap you with a truth, that is, truth as I see it today.

I want to incite a riot in the mind of this generation. I'm not concerned with whether you believe me, I just want you to hear me.

Our world is so noisy, so full of refuting and denial. Many believe there is nothing left to believe. We file into our churches and synagogues looking for nothing more than an opportunity to catch our breath before facing the uncertainties of life all over again.

The Creator wills more for us than just lungs full of air to sustain us, while we pinch our noses and hold our breath to keep from drowning in a chaotic and senseless society. He has chosen us to live. Therefore, this book is not about tragedy, death and pain or even about holding onto your faith, hopes and dreams for as long as you can before "going under." It's about "swimming"—it's about living.

I recall a story told in my days at college by an elderly gentleman during one of our student assemblies. It happened that there was a traffic accident involving two automobiles and a pedestrian. Upon the arrival of a police officer, the two drivers proceeded to argue about whose fault it was. The first driver claimed that the second driver hadn't stopped at the traffic signal, while the second driver claimed the first was driving too fast. They both were unaware that a pedestrian was hurt and bleeding in the bayou nearby. It seems they both were arguing about the right-of-way, while the victim lay in the ditch.

I did not write this book to argue doctrine or theology— I wrote it for the victim in the ditch. I wrote it for all of us who at times have floundered in a sea of questions.

I wrote it for you.

I wrote it for me.

1

Where Does It Hurt?

Nobody is free from problems. A problem-free life is an illusion—a mirage in the desert....Every living human person has problems. Accept that fact and move on....

Robert Schuller

My son Simeon burst through the door screaming at a "three alarm" level. He clutched the middle finger of his left hand. I immediately switched from father to part-time doctor and went to work. I rushed to the medicine cabinet for bandages, petroleum jelly and hydrogen peroxide. I spot-checked the tone of my voice. I had to be calm or else frighten him.

I took the finger, cleaned it off with hydrogen peroxide and searched for the injury. No cuts. He must have broken it, so I wiggled the finger from left to right, back and forth, but no breaks.

"Maybe it's a sprain?" I mumbled. I probed carefully, while all the time reassuring my tiny patient, "It's going to be alright." But in my probing I couldn't for the life of me find the injury. So I asked, "Simeon, where does it hurt?" Simeon, wiping the walloping tears from his big brown eyes, didn't respond.

I continued the interrogation.

"Is it this finger?"

"No," he replied.

"What about this one?"

"No."

"Is it your hand? Which hand?"

"No." Silence.

Let me calm down, I thought.

"Simeon, where does it hurt?"

"Daddy, it's my leg!"

A few choice words came to mind, unbefitting a preacher; for the life of me, I don't know where they came from. Could it have been the devil?

I stared intensely at my son with thoughts of torture, but he smiled and within minutes was healed and out the back door.

It's easy to cry, "Oh, God, it hurts so bad." But, where does it hurt? How many times I have pictured the old Three Stooges gag of Moe and Larry massaging Curly's arm while Curly cried out in pain, "Oh, my leg, my leg."

We don't deny hurt, but we must know where it hurts if we intend to fix it.

There are many areas of hurt with which to deal, of course, and each is just as important as the other. A poll taken by the *Houston Chronicle* in 1991 asked "What is important to you in life?" The responses were in this order:

1. Good health

2. Financial security

3. Self-esteem

What happens when these three things are not achieved? The answer is people hurt. Of hundreds of traumatic experiences, the three things that cause people the most pain are sickness, financial pressure, and rejection.

It was the summer of 1985. I was in a near-fatal automobile accident. Our church had just moved into a new building, and we were ready to conquer the world. Prior to that, we had functioned in a 6,000-square-foot upstairs office. Our church had grown to explosive proportions, and we had no more room. Through an act of God (which I will explain later), we were fortunate enough to acquire larger facilities, 25,000 square feet to be exact! This building, we thought, would ensure the growth of our congregation for at least four or five more years. I'll never forget standing before the crowd on that first Sunday. Our congregation had jumped from 120 people to over 200 in just one week, as a matter of fact, in one service alone. We were invincible!

Everything was perfect. But on my way to the new administrative offices two days later, I remember turning the corner onto the street where our new property was located. Because of the way the street curved, I did not see an oncoming pickup truck. Within seconds, just as I was about to turn into the driveway, the truck slammed into the passenger side of my 1976 Peugeot—a very small car facing a V-8 monster. The next thing I remembered was crying out, "Jesus," and tumbling over three times. After the car settled upright, I realized that I was still alive and functioning. I didn't know it at the time, but I had a broken collar bone, a very deep gash across the right side of my face and various cuts and bruises throughout my body. Through the grace of God, an unemployed paramedic was on his way to a job interview and just happened to be driving behind the pickup truck.

Immediately they pried open the left car door, and I somehow staggered out under my own power. I felt lukewarm trickles flowing down my face. What was it, perspiration? No, blood! There was a laceration extending from my right cheekbone to just under my jaw. Within minutes my secretary, who had been watching from the window of the church offices, got on the telephone and called emergency. By then other paramedics had miraculously appeared on the job.

I was put on a stretcher. My mind was still unable to sort it out. What had happened...how did it happen...was I going to live...was I going to die? In minutes I saw the words "emergency room" flash before my eyes. I was in a hospital. People were scurrying, moving fast. My body was lifted from the stretcher and placed on a cart with wheels. They rolled me into a small room and proceeded to cut away my clothing.

When the doctor walked in, the first things he did was to apply pressure to various parts of my body. He asked,

"Does this hurt?" Now when a doctor asks you whether this or that hurts, you know sooner or later he's going to touch something that will answer his question. I knew eventually he would get to the injury and create a severe pain! The question was when!

I tried to tell him, "Listen, my neck hurts, my back hurts, my shoulder hurts..." But he was determined to start from the toes up and ask the questions while he squeezed. Squeezing my feet, he asked,

"Does this hurt?"

"No."

My legs.

"Does this hurt?"

"No."

My knees.

"Does this hurt?"

"Ooooohhh, yes!"

My thighs.

"What about this?"

"Yes!"

My stomach.

"This?"

"Oh, God, yes!"

My ribs.

"And this?"

"Yes! Yes!"

Finally he got to the collar bone.

"And what about this?"

"Arrhhgg...uh huh!"

When, I thought to myself, *will this sadist ever stop?*

The question was the same with each area of my body. Why? Because the doctor had to isolate the injured area in order to treat it.

Admittedly, each human being has areas of hurt. Somewhere in our minds, our emotions or in our backgrounds are things that have caused us pain. Whether it be the loss of a loved one, something that happened in our childhood or a direction in life in which we wanted to go but were unable, there are hurt places. Maybe it was a career we wanted to start yet couldn't get off the ground level. Whatever it was, pain remained concealed until someone probed with the question, "Does this hurt?"

Isn't it interesting how as human beings we love to portray the image of Superman? We put the plastic smile on our face, hop on the stage of life and pretend that nothing is wrong. We're safe in crowds, because crowds don't know what's really going on inside.

Smokey Robinson recorded a song that said, *"Take a good look at my face, you'll see my smile looks out of place, but if you look closer, it's easy to trace the tracks of my tears."*

It doesn't matter who we are. Somewhere, something in our life hurts. And when people begin to probe with the question, "Does this hurt?" its like that doctor touching, probing and squeezing various parts of the body. We know somewhere down the line he's going to touch that sore or tender spot, and we also know we're going to let out a scream. We know we're going to cry, and we know we're going to have to admit that it hurts.

Sickness

A young man was a very faithful member of our church. Sunday after Sunday he would smile, yet I sensed a distant look about him. One day, I questioned him concerning his past. It turned out that this young man had been a star football player in high school. In his senior year he was given a scholarship. He went to college and made the varsity team in his freshman year. After college he was drafted by a professional football team. Finally the day came. The possibility of a multimillion dollar contract was imminent.

This young man had grown up in a small town. His family lived in a tiny four- or five-room house. This football contract would have enabled him to move his family to decent surroundings in a decent area of town, and he was looking forward to it. But one day while practicing, he injured his knee. When it was examined, there were major torn ligaments. In the doctor's estimation, that knee would give him problems for the rest of his life. The professional football team turned him down, and the young man came home without the contract.

Although he smiled and sometimes laughed about it, still deep inside his heart he wanted to play professional football. He knew he would never get the chance again, and not only did that rob him of a professional career, but it robbed him of his motivation and drive in other areas of his life.

I'll never forget the young man's actions while he was sitting in my home. While I talked with him it seemed as if the old demons of his past had begun to play havoc with his emotions. Weeks later he was found running and screaming down the middle of main street. He was picked up by the police, restrained and placed in a mental institution. I often have wondered what happened to him, but I do know that sickness had robbed him of his dream.

Sickness embarrasses people. Years ago I was involved in a small weekly discussion group. Several pastors and lay leaders would meet to compare notes on current issues. One of the group members had cancer, which basically had devoured one-fourth of his head. Medical science was still rather inexperienced in chemotherapy, so little was being done for him. The sores were open and bleeding, giving off a putrid stench. I tried my best to act as though I didn't smell anything, but it was hard to hide. The stench of cancer upset me to the pit of my stomach, and I fought the urge to throw up. Weeks passed, and we learned to live with it. He knew we could smell the odor of rotting flesh, even though we said nothing. He was embarrassed, yet nothing could be done.

To some people, sickness conflicts with their faith in God. People pray for other people all the time: some get healed, and some don't. How often we have read the gospels and been awed by Jesus' healing the lame, causing the blind to see, opening the ears of the deaf, stopping the hemorrhaging of a woman who had been sick for years, and then we cried out, "God heal me!" Oh, how we love these stories! But can any of these miracles happen today? Can they happen today for me? Well, they're happening for somebody! Miracles are reported on Christian television every day. But for some, it always seems to happen to someone else. Does God hear us! Does God care? Does God feel pain? Does God know that we are sick? The Bible says one thing, yet personal experience often speaks just as loud—thus we have confusion!

It costs to be sick—the prescriptions, the visits to the doctor, the little things you would not normally purchase if the illness didn't exist. Don't forget those who've experienced financial wipeout when they could no longer work or move about as they once did. Thank God for medical insurance; but even medical insurance many times pays only 80 percent of the bill.

Waking up each morning with physical sickness and pain is a living hell! When I was brought home after my car accident, I felt as though all of the energy had been drained from my body. It was even painful to sleep. For months I was confined to a reclining chair, unable to sleep in a regular bed. My wife, Saundra, literally had to pick me up in order to get me into a bathtub. The shoulder brace was painful to take off and put on. I know how it feels to be sick. I know how it feels to wake up morning after morning with pains in different parts of the body. Those who have never experienced an illness or injury can only sympathize with those who have. But when it happens to you, you know the inconvenience, the hurt and the embarrassment.

Sickness can curtail the ability to work and feed one's family. Individuals who have been injured on their jobs or forced to live on retirement income or workman's compensation feel the strain. To wake up in the morning knowing that they cannot physically provide for their families can be depressing. Watching a wife go to work, knowing that she is now the breadwinner, takes away from a man's self-esteem. It not only works on you physically, but it works on you emotionally and mentally.

Sickness robs an individual of the right to do for oneself. I know of individuals who would love to be able to go into the kitchen and cook for themselves, but because of sickness they cannot. Many would love to clean their own homes or just button a shirt or blouse, but cannot. Those who are born without limbs and do not have the ability even to put on a sock greatly desire to do for themselves rather than have someone else do for them. When you're sick, you wonder whether there is any worth to your personal life. Will you ever be whole again?

I've spoken to those who have heard the news from the doctor that they will be paralyzed for the rest of their lives. This often causes deep trauma and emotional pain.

Imagine having to survive on pain pills—a pain pill after breakfast, one after lunch, one after dinner, one before going to sleep and upon awakening. Imagine the feeling of raw nerve endings pounding, throbbing, while you hope and pray, "Oh God, let it stop!"

Sickness steals motivation and drive. Imagine getting up one morning and feeling the joints of the knees or elbows not functioning as they used to. Imagine headaches pounding day after day. Imagine not knowing what's wrong, only to go to the doctor's office and wait, wondering all the time what's wrong with me? Why is my body reacting this way? What will the doctor say? Will he be able to fix it with a pill? Will I have to live with this for the rest of my life? Finally the nurse calls your name, and the doctor says, "I want you to come back and take some tests." Now that's what you don't want to hear! If there's anything I don't like hearing doctors say, it is "I want to run some tests." What tests? What kind of tests? When a doctor says he wants to run tests it means he is looking for something. "Doctor, what are you looking for?" Then, "If you find it, are you going to be able to fix it?" If the doctor can't fix it, you slowly feel your motivation draining. What about my dreams? My goals? What about the things that I have always wanted to do? Sickness hurts physically, emotionally, mentally, socially and financially.

Most people know that a church will fill up fast when it's reported that someone who was sick has received a healing. If you want to get a crowd, advertise the fact that yesterday you prayed for someone and they were healed. The next day you will have a multitude show up. Why? Because people want to be whole. They want to be well. (Please understand that I am not saying this to demean or to downgrade healing services or meetings at which evangelists or pastors actually pray specifically for the sick; God knows we need it.)

But what about those who don't get healed? What about those who never find that "healing touch of God?" What about those who never experience relief from a withered hand or who never stand again after being in a wheelchair for 20 years? What about their state of mind? What about their emotions? What about their belief system?

The Bible tells the story of a woman who had been hemorrhaging for a number of years; she endured a constant menstrual cycle (see Luke 8:43-48). Not only was this uncomfortable, but the religious people of her day considered it to be spiritually unclean. So she lived with a religious stigma as well as something which was a physical offense to anyone around her. She was treated by so many doctors that her entire financial reserve was drained; she had spent all that she had. To top it off, the diagnosis was no cure.

Needless to say, she had lost hope; however, she heard about the man, Jesus. She sought Him out, found Him, touched Him and was healed. She would never forget the moment of her miracle, but she also would never forget what she had gone through to get there.

Rejection

If a young man wants popularity, he plays school sports. When you play school sports, the girls are going to like you, and the guys are going to think you're cool (cool means you're okay, you're a good guy, you're accepted). Did I say the girls are going to like you? They will adore you!

Well, I went out for the basketball team, and I was pretty good. I had a nice jump shot, knew how to execute lay-ups and was an all-around hustler. My hustle made up for lack of ability, but that's not bad. I had always been chosen for street teams at the playground, but I knew this would be different.

After tryouts, the coach said, "I'll post the names of those who made the team on the bulletin board." I'll never forget one week later running to that bulletin board ready to see my name. I was about to start my high school basketball career. In my mind, I already had a sweater with a school letter, a girl hanging on each arm and invitations to all of the parties. I could see myself walking down the halls of the school with everybody shouting,

"Hey, Ed, how are you doing? Good game. Man, that sure was some shot you made!" (Funny what the mind can do.) But in a split second, while reading that bulletin board I learned the difference between illusion and reality. My name wasn't on the list! I had been "cut"! Now for those of you who are not familiar with the phrase, the word *cut* means, "don't show up for practice anymore! We don't want to see you! You don't fit in with our basketball scheme!" It means there are other players who have greater skills, or they have enough players with the type of skills they need. Today, I understand that it only meant I had a greater talent in an area other than basketball. But at the age of 16, the word *cut* equaled the word *rejection.*

Rejection, "the action of rejecting; the state of being rejected; something rejected." Rejection hurts, and we all have the scars of being rejected from something or by someone at one time or another, whether it was a job or some inner circle. Regardless of the reason, we felt that we didn't measure up.

Imagine having the ability to hear all the thoughts of those who come within four feet of you. In a typical day you might hear something like this:

I was a good wife. I gave him 17 years of my life. Just because she's thin and 15 years younger, he didn't have to leave me for her. Why did he leave me? Why did he reject me?

I've worked for this company for 12 years. I was next in line for promotion, but...

Why did she choose him? I'm not bad looking...

Why didn't he invite me to go to the prom? I'm just as good a dancer as...

I could really do something special for that church. I'm a good minister. I could really help a lot of people. Why did they not vote to...

I've got the experience. Why do I need the education? I've been working in this field for 25 years, and now all of a sudden this young person comes along who has only been out of college for six months and...

Just because I have children, but no husband, should not be the reason for not getting the apartment that I wanted. Why is it that because I have children I've got to be placed in the rear of the complex? I feel as if...

I have a good job. I know my credit is good. I know that I have not always paid my bills on time, but I have always paid them...I was just a little slow. Why is it...

If only I could lose 30 pounds, then maybe she will...

This is typically what you'd hear. People experience rejection, and rejection either will drive people deeper into themselves or drive them to lash out at others.

Rejection is not new. Even Jesus Christ Himself experienced it. "He was in the world, and the world was made through Him, and the world did not know Him. He came to His own, and His own did not receive Him" (John 1:10-11). There are several other places in the Bible that say things such as "The stone which the builders rejected..." (I Pet. 2:7). and "...rejected by men..." (Isa. 53:3). Even Jesus' own people did not accept Him as the Messiah or as the Son of God.

So "hip, hip, hurrah," we all experience rejection! It is nothing new. Rejection is all around us. We can be rejected because of the clothes we wear, because we are not wearing the styles that "Paris" or the designers tell us are "in." We can be rejected because of the color of our skin, the color of our hair or the color of our eyes.

My wife, Saundra, has experienced rejection because of the color of her hair! All of her younger life was spent in a household where her sisters and mother colored their hair. To her, colored hair was normal. (I will probably be shot at sunrise for telling this.) You see, Saundra has blonde hair, and black people are not supposed to have blonde hair. I'm not really sure who made up that rule, but my wife looks gorgeous in blonde hair! Every now and then, we run into people who feel that because she is black, she should not have blonde hair. They see her hair color as a sign of being culturally dysfunctional. Now, of course, that's nonsense!

However, some consider this to be a form of rejection by your own people. Now please understand me, I know our society is not perfect, and I am aware of racism in America and throughout the world, but it's very difficult when you experience the same type of prejudices among your own people. If my wife were not as bold and strong as she is, she could go into a very deep shell, recolor her hair or cut it all off in order to please the people who reject her. It seems the people who should be standing beside us are the very ones who reject us.

If someone would just walk up to me on the street and say, "I don't like you, I reject you," I'd probably smile and say, "Fine, good, have a nice day!" But it's different when you are with the people that you love. It's when rejection comes from your own family, your own church members or people who are somehow connected with your life that you experience great hurt.

Financial Pressure

Contrary to what we think, not everybody in America has had a taste of the proverbial "pie." As a matter of fact, many don't even know that there is a pie! There actually are people in America who can't imagine how the "other side" lives. Most people live the best way they can.

People live with unemployment and underemployment. This happens for many reasons. It's very interesting that in a country as wealthy and powerful as America there are many people out of work. Large companies that deal in profits of millions and billions of dollars think in terms of cutting back numbers of workers when they want to save money. They seldom think about how layoffs will affect families, emotions, marriages and the education of children. Underemployment can happen because an employee has a lack of self-esteem or does not have enough drive, motivation or belief that he can do better. There are people working in companies who have the gifts, skills and talents to be employers themselves, but they are afraid of taking risks. There are those who are underemployed because of moral and social ills. Racism, prejudices and even "good ol' boy" networks are against them.

There are people who live on fixed incomes and Social Security. This area has always been a "burr under my saddle"! Imagine someone working all his life, paying into Social Security, waiting, hoping and believing for the day he could retire at 62 or 65. Can you imagine waiting eagerly to live off of a Social Security check? Most people don't realize that Social Security was never meant to be their only source of income after retirement, that it was only meant to supplement what they had saved up through the years. When nothing has been saved, those living on Social Security or a fixed income will always feel the strain of a weak economy.

Now let's look at the two-paycheck family. At one time in America, it was common for the husband to get up in the morning, kiss the wife good-bye and go to work, while the wife stayed home and took care of the children. She worked in the community, took care of the home and was able to welcome the husband when he came home from a hard day on the job. As the cost of living began to escalate, the wife went to work, and not just because of escalating costs, but because she wanted to do so. As technology increased, little things such as tape recorders, CD players and VCRs became the toys of the overgrown child. Americans wanted more; therefore, the average family became a two-paycheck family. But that "extra" income is swiftly becoming extinct, because both incomes have become a necessity just to live. In a two-paycheck family, it ultimately comes to the point that neither one can afford to stop working. They usually are just one paycheck away from missing a month's rent or a payment on the car.

Then there is the problem of heavy debt, credit cards and the "you can have it now" mentality. America is "up to her ears" in plastic! We work to pay off our credit card debt, yet we need our credit cards in order to buy what we want. We have to keep our credit card payments up to date, in order to keep the companies from taking the credit cards back, in order that we might be able to buy what we want. So we have to have a two-paycheck family, in order to pay the credit card debt, in order to get what we want...can you see the vicious cycle?

Let me say something at this point concerning credit cards. In one of the books I have authored, entitled *Breaking the Spirit of Poverty,* I encourage getting out of debt as soon as possible. I also comment about staying away from a lot of credit cards because of their interest rates and the ease of getting caught up in spending, enticed by television commercials, magazine and newspaper ads. But please understand, I am not an advocate of cutting up all your credit cards. I teach and encourage people to have one or two that they are able to control.

Now, of course, cash is the best way to go. But...well... let me say it this way: The only reason I started off on cash is because I could not get any credit. When I finally got a credit card, I did what most people do—I went head over heels into debt. Finally, I cut up some of them! I got rid of some of them, got out of debt and learned how to control them. (I wanted to say that so you would know there were restraints in this author's life!)

A lot of people use credit just to be able to buy their children's clothes at the start of a school year or for unexpected emergencies. Many don't have the cash, especially in black and Hispanic communities. If you look at the statistics, you'll see that the income of these groups is far below that of the majority of people in America. It is a statistical fact that the average paycheck of those within the white community is ten times that of those in the black community.

Now credit cards, of course, will not help you much in the long run, but for some they ease the pain of today. I want us to at least have an ability to see the basic needs, such as shoes for children, clothing for school, a new dress for a wife who probably hasn't had one in a while or maybe just a new set of tires to get to work. Some people can't pay cash for everything, but they do know how to control the monthly payments. They don't use credit cards just to get more things; many times they use them to be able to get the necessities in life for a price which they can pay off in a reasonable amount of time. So let's at least have some empathy.

With credit cards you may be paying higher interest, but if you can at least pay your debts every month without feeling the pinch, then you are handling your finances. This may not be the best way, but it is a way to have some of the things that you want or need without having to wait 10 or 12 years down the line.

Then there are people living from paycheck to paycheck. Now that hurts. I know it hurts because I used to live that way. Oh yes, I would have loved to be able to put a paycheck away each month. I would have loved to be a few paychecks ahead. But the reality is that many people in America live from paycheck to paycheck, and the paycheck coming next week is already spent.

Imagine going to work one day at a job you've had for the past ten years. You open up your paycheck and suddenly there is a pink slip that says, "We're sorry, but the present economy dictates that we lay you off." Talk about sudden terror? You begin to wonder, what about tomorrow? What about my family? What about food? What about shelter? Where will we live? Can I find another job? If you're over 40, *then* you begin to wonder who will hire you at your age, even though you've got the experience.

America is changing. Things are different. The economy doesn't seem to be getting any better, and even the structure of corporate America is not helping very much. There used to be a time when a person would give his entire life to a company. The goal was to find a company, get a good position and climb the corporate ladder. Time, merit and loyalty used to be virtues. There was a time when people rewarded an individual for length of service or extra hard work. But we are in an era when corporations will have a person work for them 20 or more years, and then all of a sudden they go into bankruptcy. Now he is out of a job and without benefits. So what about all the years he gave them? They say, "Well, we're sorry, there is nothing we can do; we've got to think of the company."

Now the worker is laid off or terminated; the company is dissolved. But, six months down the line, the company re-establishes itself, reorganizes, and they never hire him back. America is becoming known for corporate disloyalty; therefore, people do not work as hard, nor do they care as much about looking after the company, because they feel the company no longer looks after them.

Unemployment, fixed income, credit card debt, two-paycheck families and corporate disloyalty all affect our paychecks. Everybody from the butcher to the baker to the candlestickmaker wants a piece of the paycheck, as well as the landlord, mortgage company, banks and God knows who else. With everybody grabbing after that last piece of your paycheck, you'd think if anybody would be sympathetic, it would be God. But we go to church, and it seems that even God wants a piece of my paycheck!

The needs never cease; there is always a "cause." Now before I'm blasted by pastors across the world, let me explain a bit. I am basing this on what I hear people say! Of course, as pastors we look at it from a different perspective. We know the needs of ministry, we know the people who are hurting out there in the streets, and we know the needs for food ministry, clothing, shelter and the building of homes for the elderly. Whenever it comes to needs, even the world says go to the Church. It becomes a vicious cycle, because the world system is pumping out more poor than the Church actually has resources to handle.

In a worship service, many people are very offended when it comes time for the offering. Regardless of how nicely we say it or how low-key it is, just the mere passing of the bucket seems to be an offense to some. It's not because people don't want to give, support causes or support the things of God. I believe that deep inside people want to give, people want to help, but when there are so many hands snatching a section of that paycheck, it seems that there is nothing left for oneself. So the pressure causes us even to become a little suspicious of God. Now, of course, we would never blame God, so we use the pastor or the church as an example.

We say, "Why should I give to the church? Why should I give to charitable causes?" The reasons vary.

...you should tithe if you are a good church member.

...because you need to help those less fortunate than you.

...because missions need your help.

...because we need a new church building.

...because if you give it shall be given back to you.

This last little statement used to bother me. If I give to the church, which is to say give to God, then God will give back to me what I have given Him. But the crux of the matter is I need more than I gave to God; if I give God something, I need more than just His giving it back to me. I need it with interest! But never fear, the Bible speaks of that, and Jesus actually says when you give to God, it does come back to you with compound interest! It comes back to you running over or with an endless supply (see Luke 6:38). So we need to understand that when we hear, "...because of the homeless, the poor, the AIDS victims, Thanksgiving baskets, Christmas baskets, Fourth of July baskets, Memorial Day baskets, Columbus Day baskets..." (please forgive me for being a little facetious!), we should give.

If we don't give, we feel the guilt. We know the causes are legitimate. All we have to do is read the newspaper, and we realize that if help is to come from anywhere, it's got to come from the people of God. If anybody should be taking care of things like welfare, aid to dependent children and financial relief, it should be the Church. If anybody can make loans, help people to buy a home or get a car, I believe it should be the Church. These may be revolutionary ideas, but I believe it should happen, because the Church has the compassion. She carries the love, and she carries the trust. So, when we are asked to give financial support, we know deep inside that we should. But to be very honest with you, we are afraid, and that fear is one of not having enough for ourselves.

Many times I watch telethons. It's very interesting because I have never seen so many pledges come in for so many worthy causes. If it's a religious telethon, they will say, "We need a hundred pledges of one hundred dollars," and the phones start ringing. They say, "Keep the phones ringing. We have a pledge coming in from Sally in Florida...another one-hundred-dollar pledge coming in from Joe out of New York...another one-hundred-dollar pledge coming in from John out of New Mexico and a thousand dollars coming in from Mark in Kalamazoo, Michigan." I actually sit there in amazement, because I also have a program on television, and it seems that if we ask for five dollars, people are ready to turn us off. But then again, it's the fundraiser, or maybe it's me! Who knows? But even in secular fundraising, they show us a lot of pictures of starving children or kids who don't have homes, and we really feel compelled to give. We are told that giving leaves us with a "good warm feeling." And it does. It makes you feel good when you are able to give to a worthy cause and help someone who has less than you.

But there are many people who would tell you, "I like good feelings, but I don't need good feelings inside—I need some money!" People are saying, "If I had more, I'd give more. If I had more, I could provide for my family better. If I had more, I could keep the bill collectors from calling on my telephone. If I had more, I would not have to get up every night to check whether my car has been repossessed. If I had more, I could do more." There is a frustration in many people in America and around the world. They want to break out of the poverty cycle.

As I write this book, there has been something pertinent released in the newspapers. It seems as though the federal government is asking the IRS to stop going after the rich and the corporate giants, and instead to go after the "little people." The reason is that it will cost less to get back taxes from the "little people" than it would from the rich. Why? Because the rich have the money to fight and elude the IRS. Tell me, what is our country coming to?

In this chapter, we've touched upon the three areas that millions of Americans who were surveyed considered to be the toughest "demons" they've had to fight. But like a headache, a sudden burst of anger or a simple case of the sniffles, the sickness, rejection and financial pressure are only the symptoms of something, not the cause.

Our hurts and pains spring from many sources. Libraries and bookstores are loaded with volumes of literature that speculate on the causes. But the need today is not only to know why we hurt or where we hurt, but how to live in spite of the hurt.

Learning to live in spite of hurt involves a process. Knowing where we hurt is where that process begins. Sooner or later everyone comes face to face with sensitive areas in life, which beg to be left alone. Somewhere down the line, the untouchable is touched. It happens either by accident, through the probing questions of a friend, or by the confrontation of one's own conscience. But as painful or embarrassing as it may seem, the beginning of the process is nothing to fear. So let it happen. The journey may be difficult, but the destination is a secure and marvelous place to live.

2

When All Seems Lost

"For to me, to live is Christ, and to die is gain."

Apostle Paul (Phil. 1:21)

Once upon a time, there lived a young man and his wife. The young man had grown up in the church with a special understanding of God from the very beginning. He often remarked, "I really do not know when or how I was born again." It's just like growing up in the house of your parents: when do you know Mom is Mom and Dad is Dad? Likewise, when do you know that you know God? Although he had grown up with this unique understanding, later he publicly acknowledged his knowledge of God.

The young lady had grown up with a father who was a very strong deacon. He really should have been a preacher, based on how we view preachers today. He was very diligent in his study of the Scriptures. This was how the woman inherited her inner strength.

When they became of age, they fell in love. Often they would sit on the edge of a lake, gazing at the moon and listening to the Temptations sing, "My Girl." Unlike the other couples who necked on the local "lovers' lane" along the shoreline of Lake Erie, this young couple would talk about the things of God (most of the time!). They loved each other dearly and looked forward to a beautiful life together.

Weeks after their marriage, they decided to settle in Texas. The young man felt his call of God was somehow connected to that state (of course, his calling was later to be defined). Their first stop was Dallas, and six months later they settled in a "small town in Texas." After three and a half years, the young man knew his destiny lay elsewhere. He felt the urge to move south. So acting upon this urge, they traveled to Houston. After one year of questions and soul-searching, the young man, his young wife and now their two children took the necessary steps to start a church.

Somehow they had known all along that the church would be built. As a matter of fact, they carried that vision very deep in their hearts. They knew it would be a lot of work with a lot of pain. There would be good times, and there would be bad ones. But they were so overwhelmed with the purpose of God that the bad times could not compare with the joy that they would receive by helping to build the lives of people, perfect strangers, but people nonetheless. In the beginning, everything looked bright. The church was strong and willing to follow wherever they led. But soon, all hell would break loose.

It never fails that when things are moving along so perfectly, trouble comes. How often do we ponder this trend, trying so hard not to adopt the pessimistic philosophy of "if things are going so well, then something bad is about to happen?" How is it that we fail to grasp the words of Jesus, who told us, "In the world you will have tribulation [pressure]..." (John 16:33; see also II Cor. 1:3-8). Is it our eyes that deceive us, or do we retreat to a first-grade reading level when we touch upon these phrases? Is there some subconscious resistance to anything that carries the scent of pain? Well, whatever it is, this couple was about to come face to face with a nightmare to beat all nightmares. Just when the church was getting on its feet, they found out that their only daughter, their firstborn, had cancer.

I cannot tell you of the emotional devastation. Listening to the doctor's report was like listening to a recorded message echoing through a long tunnel. At first there was denial, then the feeling of betrayal, but the evidence and medical facts were unyielding. The doctors went on to explain to the couple that their daughter was fighting one of the rarest forms of cancer, a cancer of the soft muscle tissue, and that the only hope was to begin a strategy of chemotherapy, surgery and waiting—hoping for the best.

I know the numbness, the emptiness and the sheer terror that this couple fought so hard to suppress. I felt time stand still and the inward wish for all of this to be only a dream. It was no longer a story to be told in the third person. I could not watch them any longer. I had to take my rightful place in time. It was not happening to someone else, it was happening to me. This was my family, my wife and my little girl.

How often in our terrible times of need do we grope in darkness for at least an ounce of faith? Of course, I had exhausted every Scripture I knew. We read every passage in the Bible that dealt with healing and faith in God, but it was hard to find faith in darkness. It was hard to keep smiling, hard to hold back the tears, though somehow we did (that is, while in public).

Ultimately, the chemotherapy started (along with much prayer), and as the weeks and months passed, the tumor, which was lodged between the muscle and bone of my daughter's leg, began to shrink. You talk about rejoicing? There was plenty of it!

Unfortunately, the chemotherapy had many side effects. In some instances, it affected the kidneys, and in some, it affected the bowels. But the worst side effect was how it affected the hair. I want you to imagine a little girl who had waited all her life to grow enough hair to be able to comb it like she had seen her mother do. We soon found out it was not meant to be. The effects of the chemotherapy, "chemo" as the doctors called it, caused every strand of hair to fall out. I'll never forget when Saundra combed our daughter's hair one morning, with each gentle stroke of the comb, patches of hair began to fall out. Sheer terror etched itself on Saundra's face.

Saundra's Story

Saundra, how did you feel during that period?

I was devastated. There was an emptiness inside. There was...a pain.

How did you feel, specifically during the side effects brought on by the chemo?

Inside, it was scary. It was a scary feeling. All I had was the Word, and I stood on the Word. But I let the Word become flesh, even in every intricate part, for example, talking to veins, blood counts, chemotherapy—the terms the doctor used. My feelings were human. It was like I didn't know what I was doing. I didn't know if I was doing this right. I didn't know if I was making the right decisions. I didn't know if I was being strong enough in my faith. Uh, I didn't know. But still there was a confidence inside that we were going to pull out. And I think I had reprogrammed my mind to say that whatever we were going through, regardless of what it was, we were going to come out of it victorious in every area.

What bothered you about the chemotherapy?

I didn't know what it was. No one in our family had ever been sick, so I never knew what chemotherapy was. It was very new to me. It was very, very different. I had never heard anything about it. I did some study on it, as much as I could, and asked a lot of questions of a lot of doctors. God was very gracious in giving us good doctors and nurses to really explain to us in detail what to expect. I didn't know that they had to tell you the negative as well as the positive, and basically I took more of the negative, until I got into a habit of listening to them and taking what I needed to keep hoping and then working along with that.

I think the hair loss and the throwing up were the scariest part. It was very scary. I remember when she took her first chemo and all of the hair came out, I ran out the door. I literally ran out the door! I didn't know what to do. And to see the baldness there, I didn't know what it was. I didn't know that the medicine could do that much damage to her. Then there were Angela's feelings. I didn't know what kind of pain she was feeling, so I had to go by my own strength in the Lord to deal with it.

Ed's Story

The weeks passed, and the tumor shrank to the point that it could be surgically removed, and it was. It was time to rejoice again. But little did we know that in just a few short months we would be dealt another crushing blow. The tumor returned, only this time it had metastasized to another part of the body. The tumor was now in the chest area.

How often we complain about the stubbing of a toe, a simple headache or a small back pain. Of course, I realize that sickness is relative. A cut finger to some can cause just as much distress as major surgery to others. But some sicknesses threaten the balance of life and death. It is here we learn to be grateful for life, when we come in contact with those who are fighting just to retain it.

We were fighting for the life of our daughter. Months later we saw some light at the end of the tunnel. The doctors had given very little hope, yet they were amazed that the tumor again was shrinking. Once again, the plan was to shrink it to a certain point and surgically remove the afflicting "demon." Only this time, the shrinking tumor stopped short of the goal, and before they could operate, it began to grow again. The doctors explained at this point that there was nothing more they could do. Of course, they would try radiation and experimental drugs, but they really did not see much hope.

People ask us all the time, "How did you feel?" Probably the best answer for that would be, "How do you think we felt?" But unless it's happening to you, it never enters your thinking, and if it does, it goes out as fast as it came in. However, through the years, my wife has always encouraged me with "tell people how you feel; preachers always have the answer, but people want to know how you *feel*." Naturally, I usually argued that reasoning by pointing out, "I'm here to preach the Word, not expose my feelings." I don't know, maybe it's a combination of privacy and a "male thing."

Over the years, I've mellowed. I've learned that people need to catch a glimpse of our humanness.

Saundra's Story

There were times when you just went to the hospital and the stays were not just days but weeks. There was even one extended stay that lasted a month. How did you feel being in a hospital with other children who were dealing with the same disease?

I think it was something like 33 days, and then we had plans for the summer. We had plans for activities and things of that sort. I thought it was unfair that God would place us in a position like that. At night there was no sleep at all. It was a constant drain. I did everything possible concerning the

Word, praying, anointing with oil, Scriptures on the wall and having music playing. But the hospital stay was the scary part, because I would see children die. It was as though satan were telling me it's going to be my turn next, and she was going to die here in the hospital in those 33 days. But I didn't take that report. I rejected it, and I stood on the Word and believed God.

I remember one time when she had so much medication in her that she "fell out" in the restroom. I thought she was dead, and I called Ed and he prayed on the phone; then the doctors and nurses came and said that she had so much medication in her that she had just passed out. I thought she was dead. Now that scared me.

Another time was when they had to stick the tube into her chest to drain fluid from her lungs. That was a motherly pain. It was like I wished it was me instead of her. She stated to me, "Mommy, I'm not going to stay in here. I'm going to get out of this hospital, and I'm going to make sure that we get through this." So with her enthusiasm, the Word inside her, her strength and my strength, I think we pulled it off pretty well. But still, late in the midnight hour, praying for her and seeing her lying there is a pain that is indescribable as a mother. Not just for yourself, but you're seeing other parents going through it, and they're worse off than you are because they don't have the Lord. They don't have any kind of faith. There was a lot of ministry involved. She and I together, we would go from room to room, helping and encouraging other families and other children.

Throughout the entire sickness, what bothered you the most?

There were several things that really bothered me. One of the things was that my faith level was very strong, and the Word was very strong inside her and me, but why didn't God move when His Word says, "...by His stripes we are healed?" "...if you say to this mountain, 'Be thou removed.'..."be made whole" "...if they drink anything deadly, it will by no means hurt them." I would speak those words without any doubt, without wavering, yet it seemed that those things didn't come to pass. We would go through those side effects. That bothered me. I mean that bothered me a whole lot, a whole lot...it bothered me a lot!

What do you think was going on inside your husband? How was he functioning? How was he reacting?

Well, I think I was mad at him because he didn't react—he was quiet. I guess he didn't react the way I thought he should. To me—I don't like to use this word, I shouldn't use this word—he reacted *nonchalantly*. That sounds like he didn't care, but it seemed like that. Ed's reactions were very quiet, very subdued. Uh, the touching or the praying was very still and calm. I guess being charismatic, full gospel or whatever you want to call it, I thought his reaction should be stronger, yet his reactions were very still. He was just there. That made me very angry.

Those were his actions on the outside, what do you think was going on inside him?

I think Ed was getting to the point that he was very, very angry with God. He was very disappointed. I could feel the disappointment. Inside, it's like "Father, here's my child. I'm doing all that I can. We're working, and we're standing on the Word." Though he may have seemed angry at God, he wasn't angry at people. There was no time to be angry at other people. We always had a forgiving heart for those who mistreated us or persecuted us or said things like "You're not standing on the Word." This told me he wasn't really angry at God. There was always a sureness and a calmness and a love for people. So I knew that couldn't be it. I just knew that he felt that God knew something that he didn't know, and he was very puzzled about it, and God was not giving him the answer yet.

Ed's Story

Often we find ourselves in situations where there seems to be no hope. The apostle Paul once spoke of this when he had experienced a terrible time in Asia. He said,

Blessed be the God and Father of our Lord Jesus Christ, the Father of mercies and God of all comfort...For as the sufferings of Christ abound in us, so

our consolation also abounds through Christ...For we do not want you to be ignorant, brethren, of our trouble which came to us in Asia: that we were burdened beyond measure, above strength, so that we despaired even of life. (II Cor. 1:3,5,8)

Paul and his associates had reached a point where the pressure, conflict and problems were so devastating that they were left with the conclusion that nothing could be done. How often we echo the same feelings, whether it involves overdue bills, sickness, a child on narcotics or a marriage that is less than a marriage. Whatever the reason, in our generation many hopes are dashed against the rocks.

That's how Saundra and I felt. Throughout this entire ordeal we felt battered. Yet, remarkably, Angela had a great amount of strength and faith in God. It is interesting that it was a crisis which drove us deeper into the bosom of God. We prayed day in and day out. I would sit at the door to Angela's room, reading Scriptures such as, "I am the resurrection, and the life...."

The cancer progressively grew worse. One day Angela, while staring into space, began to talk about seeing saints in Heaven and on earth simultaneously. The figures she saw on earth were recognizable, and many of them were members of our church, while the figures in Heaven were hard to distinguish. But somehow she knew they were connected. Were these hallucinations resulting from the pain or medication? In the natural, it was hard to tell, but deep inside I knew the truth.

In the Bible, we often read how Jesus poured out His life during His last days on earth. He healed the sick, raised the dead, cast out demons, forgave those who needed forgiveness, and ultimately He was crucified and buried. Yet, He gave us a commission to go forward into the things of God, to do greater works than He ever did. So Angela took a lesson from the life of Jesus. One particular day, she was patched in by telephone to a local radio station through which she was able to pray the prayer of faith for thousands who were listening. Many people, at her request, laid hands upon their radio and experienced healing. She even gave a wonderful message to a group of young people, and out of that message was birthed a very unique teen fellowship.

As the weeks and months passed, Angela grew very weak. Upon our last visit to the doctor, we were told that the cancer had spread too far, and there was nothing they could do.

On the night of the twenty-first of December, as always, the family decorated the Christmas tree. All Angela wanted to see was the star placed upon the top of the pine tree. After the star was placed on top, she requested to go upstairs. Of course, we said, "Well, let's just wait down here for a while." But Angela, as if mustering her last bit of strength, firmly demanded, "Take me upstairs."

Thank God for television ministry and for the inventions of such things as cassette recorders. All night long, we played tapes on healing, and we were able to turn on the television and allow her to hear praise and worship music and messages that were soul shaking.

That night I couldn't sleep. So as I frequently did, I picked up the manuscript of a new book I was writing and did some work. Of course, I didn't write much. We never dreamed that December 21 would be the last time we would see our child alive. The doctors had told us that her passing would be very painful and that she would have to be brought to the hospital because we would not be able to handle the suffering. Then came Tuesday morning. It was 7 a.m.; it was dark, the wind was blowing, and there was a chill in the air. I knew something was wrong, I could feel it in the house.

Saundra's Story

Let's talk about the morning Angela passed away. What went through your mind? What was going on inside you?

I have to go back to maybe about a month before, because there was a preparing inside me. I would give Angela a bath, anoint her water with oil, and I would pray in the spirit. I don't know why I did it, but I did it. She would ask me, "Mommy, am I going to die?" I would tell her, "No!" It was just she and I and that was her time with me and my time with her. It was as though the Holy Spirit would say out of my mouth, "And if you did, so what? You would be with the Lord. What difference would it make if you did?"

The homegoing was a precious time. I went upstairs that morning to see her, as I always did. I could always see her back moving from the heavy breathing, and I could always feel her pulse. This time I didn't feel a pulse. I saw a stillness, and there was a stillness in the room. I came downstairs and told my husband to go upstairs and look. He went upstairs, looked at her, checked her pulse and said, "She's gone." I can recall that moment and that time when we were in the hallway next to her room. I can recall the words "It's over" in my spirit; it meant that the battle was over. It was like a big release. It had been like a warring between satan and us. It was like "it's over," and he didn't win anything. I was totally quiet, because I knew it was over, and we had won. That was inside my spirit. I was tired. I was not in my right mind. You know how some people can say they're in their right mind; I was not in my right mind. I think I was exhausted, I mean really exhausted.

Ed's Story

It was time for the funeral. I wished I could somehow turn back the hands of time, start all over and maybe do something different from what I had done before.

The coffin was placed in the hearse, and the hearse drove slowly to the grave site. After the coffin was taken out and laid upon those familiar ropes that I had seen while preaching so many funerals, it was time to speak the words over the body. But this time it was a body out of my own flesh. There were several pastors who spoke to the teary-eyed congregation of several hundred. Questions were rampant. Some asked why? Why do bad things seem to happen to good people? As if it were expected of me, rather than allowing someone else to do it, I took a handful of dirt, sprinkled a little on the casket and said the familiar words, "Ashes to ashes, dust to dust."

Saundra's Story

Tell me about the funeral. What were you experiencing in your mind? What was happening with your feelings? What was going on in your emotions?

I didn't have any emotions. I didn't have any feelings. I didn't have anything. I was numb.

U-WIN (You, Woman in the Now) is a cell-group concept that we founded, which ministers to a lot of women dealing with hurt, frustrations, depression, fears and insecurities. As we walked through the funeral home and saw all of our members, along with other pastors and pastors' wives, it seemed I heard the devil say, "Now you, 'you woman in the now,' what have you won? Ha, ha, ha!" I heard that very clearly, and I felt embarrassed. I did. I really did feel embarrassed. The devil was saying he won. But then I went to the casket, and I said, "Devil, you have won nothing." I really did. I said he had won nothing.

Getting into the car and going to the burial site, I was totally numb. Everything was over within a matter of minutes. I can't even recall much. All I remember is just staring into space. I saw the pink casket sitting there. There was something inside me that wanted to go to Heaven. I wanted to go get her and bring her back, but I couldn't. I knew I couldn't. But there was one moment when my husband said, "It's over." I said, "I want to see her. I want to see her body go down into the ground."

Ed didn't understand, and he told me, "No, it's
over." I said, "No, I want to see her body go into
the ground." The reason I wanted to see the casket
go into the ground was I had to symbolically let go
inside my spirit. Inside my being, I had to declare
to the devil that he hadn't won anything.

**So you are talking about watching the coffin go into the
ground, releasing something?**

Releasing self. Releasing me. Releasing everything,
who I am, what I was. I wanted to release all of
that, and when the coffin went down into the
ground, I died. When I say, "I," I mean the flesh.
When I got up, I got up new. It was like a rejuvena-
tion. It was like a rededication to my life, to my
ministry, to what I had to do as a woman of God.
This job is for real. I'm not playing. I won't play
with the devil.

But you had never played with the devil before.

You have to understand, when I say I'm not playing, I'm saying I'm exposing the inner parts where
the enemy plays games with reasoning, logic, upset emotions and other things that go on within
women. I want to deal with women who have lost
loved ones or children. I want to expose the enemy
and his tactics. I have always kept some things inside—speak a positive message, keep it positive
and never let negative things come out. I said I
wasn't going to do that anymore. Of course, the
Word is positive, but I planned on letting women

know how the enemy does what he does. I would expose the negative, uncover it and deal with it from the Word of God, rather than hide it and hope it goes away.

What changes took place in your life in the weeks, the months, after Angela's passing? What changes did you go through?

I don't want to sound superspiritual or anything, but it seems as though everything I touched made a difference. I spoke to people—things happened. Healings took place all over. I recall after she had passed, I went back to that hospital and three young men got saved, and a young girl got healed.

When I'm speaking at conferences, it seems that the message is clearer, to women as well as to men. It's easier to communicate to pastors' wives. They really take a beating.

I don't know how, but something unique would happen inside a mall, a grocery store or inside... wherever! Even little bitty things like getting a parking space in the front of a grocery store. Things just happened.

So you're saying you never had any more bad days after the funeral?

Yeah, I had more bad days. I had crying days. I had hurting days. I did not like the holidays, and I still don't like holidays. I have bad days on my birthday, Thanksgiving and Christmas. Angela loved

Christmas. But I counteract it by giving. I give out of the feeling of emptiness. I give to others, and giving to those who are less fortunate makes me happy.

Somebody once came to your church and, in a very religious way, said in front of you, your husband and your church that you had a spirit of grief and that this spirit was somehow holding back the congregation. Do you have a spirit of grief?

No.

What do you think about it? How did you feel about that?

I was furious! You can tell a person with a spirit of grief. They don't do anything. They allow their appearance to go down. They let their homes go down, their marriages are broken apart...they're just not alive. They're not doing as the Word says; they are not comforting. They are not letting Jesus be Lord of their lives. They are not helping with their other children. They are not homemakers or working somewhere to help others. A spirit of grief will pull you down emotionally.

When that person said that we had a spirit of grief and our church was going down, that was a wrong prophecy. I believe religious people must be careful of what they say. They can be very insensitive at times, that is until it happens to them. We were going on, even in the midst of our pain. So I totally dismissed it.

Do you think that religious leaders, Christians or people who claim to have the "inside track" with God can sometimes be insensitive?

Yes, a lot of leaders can be; some of them are. I hate to say it like that, but many of them are. They are not stopping, listening and waiting to hear from other leaders. They assume from previous experiences or other people to whom they've ministered that every case is the same. Everybody who has lost a loved one does not have a spirit of grief. I believe that some leaders don't take time to be sensitive and to listen to people because it is painful to listen. Yes, we must be strong and protect our faith and positive attitude, but we are human.

After experiencing what you have experienced, how has it helped you as a spiritual leader? How do you deal with people differently from these "insensitive" leaders?

When people call me, I'm going to be honest. I help the people. I do like Jesus did. I have compassion and affection for people. My goal is to heal the hurting and seek out the lost. I have more compassion for hurting people and for the lost than ever before. If someone is hurting, my compassion goes out. I will stop for a minute in the hallways of our church, regardless of how busy I am. I'll stop for a minute and say, "No, I've got to minister to that person," Because I'm not so big that I just brush people off by giving some pat answer like, "Oh, here, God bless you, Honey. God will bring you through, you just keep on praying." No, I don't do that; I stop right there and listen to them and share with them insight about what they're going through. People want to know you understand their pain. They want to know how to get through the next day and what's going to happen the next day. I believe God has given me an answer to give to others, so I give it.

There was a woman who came to our church, whose daughter had died three days prior. We had a U-WIN (You, Woman in the Now) mass rally, and her husband was there. Usually at our rallies, there is nothing but women. But we brought that husband and that wife up to the altar and prayed for them. The lady cried in my arms and later said, "This feels so good." The reason why she said it felt good was because I squeezed her, hugged her and held her in my arms as though she were a baby. I felt the love of Jesus coming out of me. After that, I was able to minister to her and share with her what, step by step, was going to take place, such as taking her daughter's clothes out of the closet. Her husband said it was nobody but God, for me to be there. That's compassion. That's love, and that's what Jesus wants us to do, even in the midst of our depression. God wanted me to touch her and pull her out of it. I'm going to continue to do it.

Looking back on it all, how do you feel about your faith in God? Your belief? Has it changed? Has it increased? Has it diminished? What has happened to your faith, your trust and belief in God?

For a couple of years, I kind of felt my faith or my belief was going downhill. When I say downhill, I mean it was like I didn't know what God was doing. But I went back to a Scripture, and after Angie's homegoing, I think I understood it a little bit more: "So are My ways higher than your ways, and My thoughts than your thoughts." I keep that in my little promise chest box. I trust Him, I believe Him, and I'm confident and sure that I'm not what I'm going to be. I know I'm going to become greater in Him, and I'm going to go from glory to glory. But one thing I do know, I am not God; He is God, and He knows more than I know. With as much Word that is inside me, I can stand. I can sit here all day and give you Scripture after Scripture, but that's not what we're talking about. We are talking about our inner man and how we feel. If anybody knows Scripture, I know it backward and forward. I'm married to a preacher! But one thing I do know in my "knower," and that is His ways are higher than Saundra's ways, and His thoughts are higher than Saundra's thoughts, and He knows more than I know.

One thing I do recall as a mother is what I thought I had lost. Angela was a housekeeper. She kept the bills, she kept the kitchen, she knew what was missing in the kitchen. You miss that as a mother. She knew what Eddie needed, and she knew what Daddy needed; she was a homemaker. We baked cookies. We went to the mall. We went shopping for her prom dress for her ninth-grade prom. All of those kinds of things get to you.

She wasn't just my daughter, she was my friend. She kept me up to date on certain things and the issues of teens. Angie was always there to encourage the teens of our church and to share with them the things that they needed to know and for what to be grateful. I miss her. I miss my friend. I miss my buddy. I miss talking to her, and that's painful. That, I think, is going to take a while for me to kind of...you know...get myself together.

Sometimes I get jealous when I see parents with their daughters, and stuff like that. But I've learned how to deal with that. That's where I take my faith, apply the Word and stand on God's Word concerning that area.

Are you stronger now to meet the challenge of ministering to other people?

Oh, yes, I'm stronger to meet the challenge. I do it every day. You learn to do it constantly.

From Lowlands to Mountaintops

The night before Angela passed away, I quoted the Scripture over her, "I am the resurrection, and the life...," but there was a look upon her face that said, "Not now, Daddy, not now." I had to strengthen my belief in the existence of another place, another dimension.

I had gradually accepted the fact that she was tired and weary of going back and forth to hospitals. As a pastor, I feel the hurts of every church member, but this was not just a member, it was my daughter. Caring for the sick is exhausting. You don't realize it while you're doing it, but utlimately it catches up to you.

It was my wife, Saundra, who displayed strength. We had moved into our then new sanctuary, and one week after our first service, I was in an auto accident (see Chapter 1). Besides caring for me and taking Angela to the hospital, she had to look after the business of the church, the preaching and the teaching. To this day, I applaud her courage, strength and determination; these are the reasons God has set His seal upon her.

Together we went through the stages of grief and anger. We lashed out at each other, but somehow through the grace of God, we were bound closer to one another than ever before.

I had preached healing, victory and deliverance, only to have to walk through the valley of the shadow of death myself. We were aware of the Scripture that said, "...weep with those who weep," but now our friends and congregation were weeping with us. I was also thankful for the many pastors who stood with us and helped with the healing process.

Somebody once commented, "Ed, you and your wife really have a lot of courage and faith." Faith? Faith? I didn't feel I had anything. I felt as though somebody had ripped my guts out.

My child was gone, and there was nothing I could do to bring her back, so I decided to just get away, leave the city. How far should we go? As far as my gas card would take us! At the time, Alaska was not out of the question, but instead we headed for the Colorado Rockies. We had to get to a high altitude and feel the numbing cold.

I found the tallest mountain I could get to, and wearing a loose jacket, I found a spot in the snow, dropped to my knees, and rather than question God, I began to worship Him. I felt no emotions, received no revelation, gained no great insight. I felt nothing, no comfort, only the numbing cold. We didn't pray, we just worshiped. It's easy to worship God or go to church when your life is under control. The difficulty comes when life gets out of control.

I had driven to Colorado, first of all, to get away. Secondly, I wanted to travel as far as I could until I exhausted myself. Thirdly, I wanted to see something larger than myself. I had to be reminded that God was still in control.

I went on to Grand Canyon National Park, where my family stood on the edge of the north rim looking out into the vastness. I saw the vivid colors of the valley mixed with the winter-white snow. We gazed into a carved wonder of the world. Later we held each other and cried out, "Lord, here we are. We have nowhere else to go. We don't know what to do, but we are still going to trust and love You. Help us!"

Leaving the Grand Canyon, we finally ended up in Los Angeles, California. There, we were honored to be able to sit for a few minutes at the feet of two wonderful people, Dr. Fred Price and his wife, Betty. I'll never forget the words of strength and encouragement from Betty, when she looked straight in our eyes and said, "You must go on, for what does it matter whether we live or die, for to live is Christ and to die is gain." We then were ushered into the office of Dr. Price.

We already knew of the experience he had had with the tragic death of his son. I had watched this man on television for years, listening to his words and trying to understand his heart. Now, like a father, he questioned me and wanted to know how much I trusted in the Word of God. Did I stand upon the Word? Had I been in the Word long before Angela's sickness occurred? He took me through the entire journey of my experiences in God. For a moment, just for a moment, I saw the tears in his eyes, feeling our hurt and pain. To many he may seem arrogant and cold on television, but he is a man of great compassion, love, faith and courage. He told me three important things that I now call a "formula for victory." He said,

1. Have another child.

2. Declare to satan that he cannot touch the lives of your other children.

3. Go back and kick the devil in the "you-know-where."

Then, like a father, he opened up his arms and embraced me. I could feel the release of the pain. It was then that I truly understood, "...they will lay hands on the sick, and they will recover."

Healing is not always placing the palm of your hand upon someone's head. Many times it's taking people in your arms and releasing them from the pain, releasing them from the hurt and from all the tools that the enemies of our soul would use to destroy our lives.

He also reminded me that I had a choice: I could either give up or go on. When we walked out of his office, we chose to go on. After staying a few more days with some very close friends, we realized it was time to go back home. So we began the journey, not knowing what would await us, but whatever would happen, we knew God was there.

Upon returning home, we did not feel like walking into the church where we had given eight years of our lives. We did not know how the people would react, but God already had laid the groundwork. There was an anniversary celebration going on in town for Pastor John Osteen. While attending the conference, we received the encouragement and love of Pastors John and Dodie Osteen. Also, there were people such as Steven and Joy Strang and Carl and Joyce Strader who opened their loving arms. We will never forget them.

Then there was a man named John Meares from Washington, D.C. He wanted to see our church facilities by way of a side trip. Yes, there was a hesitation to go back into the building that we knew we must face, but we went because Bishop Meares wanted to see it. As we pulled up to the grounds, we got out of our cars, and Bishop Meares walked through the door with us. He took each step with us, constantly pointing with his finger out of every window, saying, "You've got to build, you've got to go on. Look around, what you see is the Kingdom of God. What you're doing is Kingdom work; the Kingdom will come on earth as it is in Heaven."

Our doubts and fears were being broken. He confirmed the statement earlier given to us by Dr. Price and related the Bible story of David, who had experienced the passing of a child, saying with the force of a command, "Have another child." Within two months, my wife had conceived in the midst of the trauma. The doctors had said she would not be able to conceive for a while, yet she did! At the writing of this book, along with our 14-year-old son, Eddie, we have a 3½-year-old son, Simeon Raphael.

It may sound as if we handled this emotionally charged situation perfectly. Don't let me deceive you. These were some very difficult times, and we experienced more in the days to come.

We had to drive by the cemetery every day, just to get to our office complex. We held our heads up high and kept driving, many times never turning our attention, but at other times forcing ourselves to look, facing our fears and going on.

Then came the prayer lines. For about a month, it was hard for me to pray for the sick. I honestly had thought that I would never do it again. But people with cancer, tumors, high blood pressure, heart problems, even others who were bereaved, needed prayer. I thought I had it figured out—I refused to lay my hands on anyone.

I look back now and wonder why. Maybe I was afraid it wouldn't work? Maybe I feared their sickness would return, and I would somehow be blamed? I know the healing power comes from God, but somehow I had connected it to myself. Maybe I feared loss of credibility and ultimately loss of confidence among the people. If God would not heal my child through the laying on of hands, what made me believe He would heal anyone else? The experience was just too fresh.

About a month and a half later, I realized I could not allow those fears to get in the way. I remembered the story of the apostle Peter, who had just finished a victorious ministry on the shores of the Sea of Galilee. Jesus had instructed the disciples to go to the other side, while He Himself went into the mountains to pray. But when the disciples got to the middle of the sea, a great storm arose. The winds were blowing, the rains were falling, and the disciples were about to perish in the storm. Suddenly, through the darkness the lightning flashed like a strobe light, illuminating the image of Jesus walking upon the water. They cried out in fear, "It is a Ghost!" How interesting that they did not know who He was. They immediately responded from the fears of their past, their superstitions and stories they had heard as children about ghosts and disembodied spirits. Often when adverse circumstances arise in our lives, we fall back upon the fears of the past.

Jesus immediately said to them, "Be of good cheer! It is I; do not be afraid" (Matt. 14:27). From that passage, I learned something about how to conquer fear. Peter, in the midst of his fear, called out to Jesus, "Lord, if it is You, command me to come to You...." Jesus said, "Come," and Peter stepped out of the boat and began to walk on the water. We've always preached that Peter walked on the water, but in reality he walked on the word *come*. Peter walked on the word of Jesus. When Matthew recorded it in his gospel, he had seen Peter on the water, but in reality it was the word of Jesus that held him up. He was able to walk on the word because "...faith is the substance of things hoped for, the evidence of things not seen" (Heb. 11:1). Peter walked on the unseen. The Word of God is invisible to the natural eye in our dimension, but in the dimension of God, the Word is very tangible.

Peter overcame his fear and stepped out of that boat, trusting that God would do His work. But Peter, while walking on the water, diverted his attention from Jesus to the storm and began to sink. He cried out, "Lord, save me!" Of course, Jesus immediately saved him from drowning, but the last Scripture of that particular passage says that after Jesus saved him, they walked back to the boat, got in, and the storm ceased. This tells us that when Jesus walked Peter back to the boat, He did not stop the storm, but He walked Peter through it. It was not until they got back into the boat that the storm ceased.

So what did I learn? I learned that in the midst of storms, Jesus is there. Storms can never be so bad that God is affected by them. We are called to be overcomers or to "come over" things. God will never alter His plans because of satan's devices. Whether it is hurt, bereavement, sickness, poverty, drug addiction, family squabbles, the loss of a job or ordinary depression, God sticks to the script! Jesus is always there to walk with you through the storm and back to the boat.

It was in the middle of my fears that I made the decision to pray for the sick. Praying for the sick does not require you to feel a spiritual or an emotional rush. We are called only to do what God said, "...lay hands on the sick...." Their recovery is the decision of God.

Giving Is a Secret to Healing. How many times have we heard the quote "Give, and it will be given to you: good measure, pressed down, shaken together..." (Luke 6:38)? When we quote this Scripture, most people use it in connection with money. But the Scripture says, "Give, and it will be given to you..." which means *whatever you give*, it will be returned to you in good measure, pressed down, shaken together and running over.

Praying for Others Is a Secret to Healing. When we pray for others, something miraculous happens to us, something is given back.

I remember a few months ago I had the opportunity to perform the wedding ceremony of one of the young ladies on my staff. Her name is Ann. Ann and her fiancé, Jim, had been very faithful in ministry. Ann is the daughter of a minister, and I'm quite sure her father wanted her to remain in the city where they lived and to work with him, yet she found her destiny working with us. To Ann's father, it was a type of loss, but to us, it was a gain. So we took her under our wings and treated her as our own daughter. At the wedding, one of the strangest things took place. As I stood in the pulpit before the couple, I realized that Ann's skin tone was the same as Angela's. She was young and beautiful. She had been raised up within our own congregation. Her natural father had a daughter who was now faithful in the work of God, working in the ministry and carrying the good news of the gospel of the Kingdom to the ends of the earth. At the wedding, the Lord allowed me to perform the ceremony "in proxy" for what I might have experienced with my own physical daughter. As I gave out, healing flowed into me.

Dr. Joyce Brothers, a renowned psychologist, did an interview with Ron Stone of Channel 2 in Houston. Her husband had died, and she was relating how to deal with the grief.

> When asked "How long did it take to get over it?" Only three months, four months, five months after his death, you thought, *I'm never going to be alright again*, didn't you?
>
> She replied, "And there are times that I feel the same way even today."
>
> That's my question. Does that go away, too?

It never goes away. I spoke to John Walsh, who is the father of Adam Walsh who was murdered. I spoke to him two years ago, and 14 years after the death of his son, he was still grieving. The pain lessens. The edges soften. But it never goes away completely. And I guess everybody has some pain in their life, some loss, whether it's a loss of a child or parent; some people even grieve over the loss of a pet.

The tough times, of course, as you know, are holidays and anniversaries and so on. What we've done, we all meet—my daughter, son-in-law, grandchildren and extended family—everybody meets at our farm for Thanksgiving, for the Hanukkah/Christmas time, and we will go around the table with each person reminiscing about the person who is gone, by telling stories, funny things that have happened, sad things that have happened, and in that way, he is part of our lives.

The way you forget is by having more joy in your life, more new, pleasant experiences that begin to soften it. For me, I take my grandkids, and continue to take my grandkids, one at a time, on adventures. For others, it might be going back to school. Many colleges and universities today welcome older people who come there for the pleasure of learning, so they really learn.

In God We Lose Nothing

I have spoken of loss, but in reality, Christians lose nothing. Yes, death is very rude. Death is an interruption within the "sentence" of life. Death gives no warning—just an interruption. But how comforting it is to know that Christ came to put a halt to interruptions. We have learned through the words of the apostle Paul that:

Inasmuch then as the children have partaken of flesh and blood, He Himself likewise shared in the same, that through death He might destroy him who had the power of death, that is, the devil, and release those who through fear of death were all their lifetime subject to bondage. (Heb. 2:14-15)

Through His resurrection, Jesus Christ has set free those of us who fear the interruption of life. Death has been conquered by Him. Have we forgotten that God Himself did not spare His own son, but allowed Him to go through the pain and torture of crucifixion? Pain was involved, but there was a purpose in the midst of the pain. The Scriptures tell us that Christ became the firstborn among many brothers. The word *many* encourages us through the fact that, as Christ conquered death, so we as believers who trust in Him also conquer death. All that God has invested in you cannot and will not be lost.

Unfortunately, some people believe that after we have fulfilled our purpose on this planet, all of the education, knowledge and wisdom we have gained will somehow be lost. But God is not a God of loss, He is a God of profit. Death merely interrupts our purpose on planet earth, but we will continue with all of the gifts, abilities and talents that God had given us in life. No, we do not lose through Christ! After all, death is not a permanent interruption. "For we who are in this tent groan, being burdened, not because we want to be unclothed, but further clothed, that mortality may be swallowed up by life" (II Cor. 5:4).

Death is merely a slight pause in order to accommodate a wardrobe change. We will never be without a body, and we will never be without the faculties that will allow us to continue the will and the plan of our Creator. If all God has put in us these many years is meaningless, then what God has invested is all but lost. As I said before, God is not a God of loss, He is a God of profit, and the work He has begun in you will continue, because it is God's nature to win.

Yes, sometimes I stare out windows and feel the warm tears stream down my face. There are times that I look back and remember the joys along with the pains. But it is at these moments I look ahead and remember that "...to live is Christ, and to die is gain" (Phil. 1:21). For we do not sorrow as others do. Of course, we sorrow; but I repeat, not as others, because we have a hope within that is beyond this life. We continue on. And all that God has invested will ultimately yield a harvest. Just as a seed placed in the earth seemingly goes away and later gives birth to a plant, so we are assured that, in time, all we have planted will come back again, bringing with it more than it was.

According to the apostle Paul, we will receive a new body, a body which will be the fulfillment of the body which has always been a mere shadow of that which is to come. We shall receive a body that will continue to work and house the investment of God into and throughout eternity. We were not born to die, but born to live and live eternally. After all, it will take eternity to finish the great plans of a great Creator.

3

Now Where Did I Lose My Faith?

Losing faith in a childish understanding of God is not the same as losing faith in God.

Harold Kushner

It had been about two and a half years since a few of the guys left the fishing business in order to work for a stranger in town. This man seemed to have all the right answers. I was one of his followers. My name is actually unimportant.

I'll never forget the day when, while He was training His newly recruited apprentices, crowds began to form, and He was surrounded by hundreds. Since those in the rear could barely see or hear Him, He decided to use a natural sound system— the lake behind Him; so in order to make it work,

He asked to use my boat. I was pretty tired from fishing all night long, and I was frustrated because the fish weren't biting, so I didn't feel like untying the boat again, rigging the sails and pushing it back out into the water. But this strange new teacher just asked to be pushed out a little. He wanted to move out just enough to keep the crowds at a certain distance, ensuring that everyone could see and hear clearly. So why not? I did it. Besides, what difference did it make? Teachers come and go. It wasn't hurting me. He might even pay rent!

He began to teach the crowds while I was mending my nets. I was trying not to pay any attention, but every sentence captured my thoughts. Every word He spoke did not just fall upon my ears, but went deep inside my mind, piercing everything I was. I don't remember asking Him any questions, yet He had all the answers. This teacher was different. He knew what to say to ordinary people. Not only that, but He was also an expert at handling religious people. He not only spoke well, but He backed up His words with miracles.

I'll never forget when He was invited to a wedding reception. It was nothing unusual, nothing big, but the bride and groom had run out of wine. (If you knew anything about wedding receptions in our part of town, you know it was taboo to run out of wine!) His mother came running to Him, saying, "Son, they've run out of wine." Now we didn't understand why she would even go to Him in the first place. We didn't expect Him to run out and buy anything. We just sat, watched and enjoyed the festivities. Then He said something very puzzling. "My time has not come yet." But as if changing His mind, He turned to His mother and said, "Tell them to bring Me some pots and have them filled to the top with water." Immediately, with a smile on her face, she rushed and told the servants of the house, "Get some pots, fill them with water, and whatever He tells you to do, do it!"

As they were filling the pots, this teacher called the couple in, and the guests began to drink the water. We then realized that the most incredible thing had happened, it wasn't water they were drinking, it was wine! Even the governor who had been invited to the reception said, "Why would you save the best wine until last?" This teacher had turned water into wine!

If you think that's a miracle, wait until I tell you about my mother-in-law. She was very sick. I'll never forget when He came into the room. He did not have any magic potions or say any magic words. He merely touched her and commanded the fever to go. My mother-in-law got up from her bed and began to cook.

From that point on, the people came to see Him from miles around. They came sick and left well.

A blind man who met Him on a road called out to Him, "Sir, wait." Because the crowd was so thick, the blind man almost didn't get through. "Have mercy on me *now!*" he cried. That's when I saw another side of the teacher. He stopped, turned, looked at him, spat on the ground and made some sort of clay. He then placed it on the blind man's eyes and told him to go wash at a local pool. We left, but the reports were that the man came back seeing!

I also remember the day He walked into a place that was loaded with sick people looking for a miracle—blind people, lame people. There were even those who had lost the strength of their limbs. Not being insensitive or unmerciful, He passed by all of them and focused His attention on a specific man who was lame and had been there for 38 years. "Do you want to get well?" the teacher asked. At first the man tried to give an excuse.

"Do you want to get well?" the teacher asked again. The words He used are branded in my memory. "Rise, take up your bed and walk." The man walked away! He actually walked away!

I watched the teacher feed the hungry. I watched bread and fish multiply in my hands before my very eyes! We started off with a little and ended up with more than when we had started. I watched a mother receive back a son who had died. I watched as a man saw his daughter raised back to life.

If you think I'm making all this up, remember that boat I told you about, the time He wanted to use my boat? Well, He told me to go back out, but this time to fish in deeper water. To be honest with you, I thought He was a little off His rocker, but I did it. I caught so many fish that my nets broke, and I had to call those who were in business with me to come and help me take in the load.

We saw so many things that we can barely remember them. It takes all of us who followed Him to remember everything He did. And He did not keep the power to Himself, He gave some of it to us, and we did as He had done.

One night He told us to get into the boat and go to the other side of the lake. He promised to meet us there, because He was going to teach in another city. When we got halfway to the other side, a storm arose. It was a vicious storm. The winds were blowing harder than I had ever felt them before. The rain was coming down, and the waves were beating against the hull of the boat. I thought we were going to die. Then one of the guys shouted out, "Look, coming toward us, it's a ghost!"

As I turned, I was startled just as the rest, but I kept staring. The figure moved closer, and I realized it was the teacher. I shouted out to Him, "If it's You, let me do what You are doing." "Come," He said.

I stepped out of the boat, and as He, I walked on the water. I felt as though I could do anything! The water no longer felt like water. I could feel the power under my feet. It was as though I were walking on a sponge. I couldn't see it, but something was lifting me, not from the bottom up, but from the top down, pulling me up. There was a gravitational pull drawing me onward as I stared into His eyes and walked toward Him. But then, something happened. I looked around and noticed the storm. I began to fear drowning, and then the power left. I began to sink. It only took a few seconds for the water to just about cover my head. I knew I was going to die, and all I could do was cry out, "Lord, save me."

Then He grabbed me by the hair, pulled me out and said, "Where is your faith?" Something happened deep inside me that night, something happened in me that would change my life forever.

Of course, this could have been written by any one of the disciples who followed Jesus. Naturally, this little dramatic story is paraphrased, but the paraphrase is based on fact. The words just have been shifted to help your twentieth-century ears.

Have you ever lost something that you knew was not lost, but just out of sight and out of place? Well, I'm an expert at that, especially with car keys. It never fails. When I walk through the door, I'll lay my keys down, do something else, and a few hours later when it's time to leave again, I'll go into the kitchen searching for my keys. But somehow, they have miraculously disappeared! I firmly believe that there are car keys "munchkins!" These little creatures are probably, oh, about two inches high, and they have the strength of a 220-pound man. I believe that they are placed in every home and apartment, and their only function and purpose in life is to take car keys, place them somewhere else and spend time laughing at the person who is searching for them! Well, if these munchkins do exist, they have been laughing at me for years. When I prepare to walk out the door, the first question that comes out of my mouth is predictable.

"Saundra-a-a...where are my keys, Honey?"

Saundra replies, "What did you say?"

"I said where are my keys?"

"I don't know, where did you leave them?"

"I left them right here on the kitchen table. I know I did."

"You couldn't have. If you had, they would be there."

"Saundra, I know I left them here on the kitchen table. I can't find them anywhere. Where are my keys? Did you move them? Did you put 'em anywhere?"

"Try looking in the dining room."

"I've already checked."

I then search diligently for my keys, actually believing that my wife and children (and of course, the little munchkins) have conspired to keep me from traveling in my car. I continue to search, and I finally check the bedroom. Sure enough, there are my keys on the dresser (where I left them).

"Did you find your keys, Honey?" Saundra shouts.

"Oh...uh...yes!"

"Where were they?"

"They were just where I left them."

I feel stupid every time that happens.

In the story of creation, after Adam and Eve had eaten the forbidden fruit, the voice of God asked, "Adam, where are you?" Adam had hidden from God. But can you imagine God Almighty, who knows everything, asking "Where are you?" Now this has to be one of the most paradoxical sections of Genesis. Everybody knows God is everywhere, God sees everything, God knows everything.

It's almost as though Adam had been hanging around the wrong tree, got a taste of the wrong fruit, hid himself in a bunch of bushes, and then poor God didn't seem to know where His new creation was, so He wandered aimlessly through the garden unaware and wondering, *Now, where is Adam? I know I made him out of the dust of the earth, set him over here, and it was only a few moments ago that I brought the animals to him to name. Now all of a sudden, I've lost him.* "Adam, Oh, Adam! Where are you?"

Now, of course, I've used a little tongue-in-cheek, because God knew where Adam was all the time. God did not need to find Adam. Adam needed to find himself.

How often do we read the words of Jesus, "O you of little faith...if you have faith as...where is your faith...great faith...?" Throughout the New Testament we read these words. We are reminded not only of the quantity of faith, but also of the quality of faith.

When Jesus asks the question, "Where is your faith?" does He actually expect human beings to tell Him? Can you imagine Peter walking on the water, then all of a sudden sinking, and Jesus pulling him out, asking, "Peter, where is your faith?" Then imagine Peter answering, "Well I had it here a minute ago. I think it was in my left pocket. No...it must be in my right pocket. Oh, Jesus, were did I leave it? Oh, no, wait, I left it on the kitchen table before we got in this boat. If it had not been for this storm, all of this wouldn't have happened, so wait right here, Jesus, until I run home and get it!"

Now of course, that's a silly scenario. *God does not ask questions because He's looking for information.* Whenever God asks a human being a question, either the person is in deep trouble or God is trying to "jump-start" his overall perception about something.

If God ever asks you a question (by the way, when God talks, His voice sounds like yours only with more common sense!), consider yourself to be on a witness stand, being cross-examined by the greatest defense lawyer in the universe. I would advise you to tell the truth, the whole truth and nothing but the truth, so help you God. And tell the truth quickly. I guarantee it's less painful that way.

Several years ago, I met a lady who was scheduled to sing at a church function. The church was packed. I mean packed! The woman wore a bold-patterned, sky blue dress and a very large hat decorated with artificial daisies. This woman looked like she could sing. As the musician sat at the piano and began to ripple his fingers across the keys, the woman walked to the microphone, folded her hands opera style and held her posture. As we all sat in anticipation of awe, she opened her mouth, and then there was "vocal horror!" If there had been an empty wine glass in front of her, we all would have been covered with glass from the front to the last pew. I mean her voice was beyond terror! Have you ever listened to someone writing on a blackboard with a brand new piece of chalk? Well, you could feel every vibration and every screech of her voice to the pit of your stomach. I'm quite sure she was a great Christian and loved the Lord, but there was one thing God had not given her. He probably gave her a great amount of everything else, but He did not give her a voice!

"Did you enjoy my solo?" I heard her ask the person in front of me, and I tried to pretend that someone was calling me from the rear of the church. I looked back, but no one would catch my eye. I couldn't leave. I was trapped! Finally, she turned to me, and I heard the identical question reverberate as if we were in the twilight zone. "Pastor, did you enjoy my solo?" A thousand thoughts went through my mind. I hesitated and then answered, "It was wonderful, wo-o-o-nderful!" (Wheeew!)

About five minutes later I heard that old familiar voice ask me the question, "Why did you tell her that?" God knew why I had said what I said. There was no sense in trying to pull a fast one, because God knows everything. He sees everything and hears everything. (He even heard her voice!) I ignored the question, choosing to believe it was my own conscience. But then I heard it again, "Why did you tell her that?" It shook me.

Now why did God ask me that question? Because God didn't know the answer? No, of course not. The question was not intended to provide God with information; it was intended to cause me to decide how I would handle incidents like that in the future. Would I tell a story (lie! lie! lie!), or would I somehow develop a way of telling people the truth?

I've been a musician and songwriter for nearly 34 years, and because of my visibility in the music field locally, that false encouragement possibly could have caused the woman a lot of heartache and maybe even a lot of money in the future. God could have given me words of honesty. It may have shocked her, but it would have saved her much future heartache.

God asks questions to make us come face to face with our own degree of honesty and integrity. So when God asks, you, "Where is your faith?" He's not trying to find out where it is, He's trying to get you to look deep within yourself and sort out your relationship with Him.

The "losing" of faith cannot be equated with the losing of God. Rabbi Harold Kushner in his book, *Who Needs God*, says, "Losing faith in a childish understanding of God is not the same as losing faith in God." The New Testament writer Paul says,

When I was a child, I spoke as a child, I understood as a child, I thought as a child; but when I became a man, I put away childish things. For now we see in a mirror, dimly, but then face to face. Now I know in part, but then I shall know just as I also am known. (I Cor. 13:11-12)

The phrase *when I was* indicates a previous state of being. *When I became* indicates a present state that had evolved from the previous.

The apostle Paul goes on to further explain the process of development. He says, "...now we see in a mirror, dimly [distortedly]...." In his time, mirrors were made of highly polished metal; they did not have the visual perfection of mirrors today. You could see the image, but the image was not a true image, because of the shape and surface of the metal. In Paul's life, one of the areas that was in development was faith. He says, "And now abide faith...." Even though his faith had been childish and immature, it was still faith. Faith does not disappear. It may mature or remain stagnant, but it doesn't disappear.

I'm reminded here of a man named Jonathan. Now Jonathan was a real go-getter. If you were to walk into his office you would see slogans, mottos and words of wisdom, all designed to keep Jonathan "pumped." Jonathan considered himself to be a man of very strong faith. He had a good job, stable income and a very bright and prosperous future. If you asked him, "Jonathan, why does it seem that everything you touch turns to gold?" Jonathan would reply, "It's my faith in God. I believe that God supplies all of my needs in every situation."

Unfortunately, due to a series of bad business deals, economic recession and loss of income, Jonathan fell on hard times. This devastated him. He couldn't eat. He couldn't sleep. He even began to doubt whether God was with him. He tried everything he knew to do. He searched the Scriptures, prayed hours each morning and even boosted his attendance at church, but nothing seemed to be happening. Of course, we realize that something was happening, but not what Jonathan had expected to happen.

Jonathan soon came to the conclusion that not only had he lost some very important accounts, but he had lost his charmed life. Eventually, this setback caused him to question everything he believed. He questioned the Scriptures he had memorized, his confessions of faith and the slogans and mottos on the wall. So Jonathan stopped praying as often. His local church attendance slowly tapered off. Jonathan had all the symptoms of a man who had lost faith in God. He was hurt.

But then a series of events took place. With a failing career, lack of motivation and overdue bills stacked up to his forehead. Jonathan forged some new techniques of managing his life style. He learned to live on only half his previous income. In time, he received a new surge of hope for his career. His motivation returned, and eventually he paid off his overdue bills. By the way, Jonathan started praying again and returned to church. He even put his words of wisdom back upon the wall (not all of them, just a few).

Here's my question: Did Jonathan lose his faith in God? Not really. But Jonathan did lose his immature understanding of how God provides.

You see, we change daily. Our concepts mature, our perceptions broaden, and we learn daily.

Every now and then, old friends would call me and say, "Hey, remember me? We were schoolmates. We used to play basketball and party together." I replied, "Oh, yes, I remember you now." They responded, "Well, I'm still the same old guy you knew in high school, ha, ha, ha!" It was at that point I wondered whether I needed to renew the acquaintance.

I realize when we use clichés like "I'm still the same," it's because we don't want our friends to think we have forgotten our background. But the indwelling of Christ changes clichés. To say that I'm the same old guy I was is an indictment upon the Christ that dwells within. He does change us from glory to glory. What was fact yesterday often becomes questionable today. What we consider fact today, we may choose to forget tomorrow. Now this does not mean we lose our faith, it only means we're growing up.

The other day, our son Eddie, walked through the door along with his younger brother, Simeon. Simeon ran halfway across the room, *jumped* into my arms and yelled, "Hi, Daddy!" Eddie *strolled* across the room, gave me a nice big hug and said, "Hi, Dad." Now I can remember when my older son reacted to seeing me just as my youngest had, but that was years ago. Just because my oldest son is not reacting the way he used to does not mean that I've lost my son. On the contrary, it only means he's growing up. I'm not losing him, I'm merely watching him develop.

To feel that we have "lost faith in God" hurts, but we can survive. As a matter of fact, we do survive! God does not fall from His throne because we fail to understand things. In some ways, I think He smiles at it. I am convinced that if we let Him, He will take us far beyond our present lack of understanding.

It's the moment when we're really unsure about what step to take that we wonder whether or not God is around. It's when we've had one of the biggest arguments of our marriage, and our spouse brings up the question, "Why don't we get a divorce?" that we wonder whether it's all worth it. It's when we thought we had enough to financially make it to the next week, only to realize we don't, that we question the benefits of having faith. To be honest, sometimes you don't want to be strong, you just want to have a pity party and cry. This is what the apostle Paul calls "looking through a mirror dimly." It's when we feel we've lost God. But relax, we never really lose God. God's personality is too large and awesome to lose.

Second Corinthians 4:17 says, "For our light affliction, which is but for a moment, is working for us a far more exceeding and eternal weight of glory...." I know that sounds good, but to be honest with you, who likes affliction, regardless of its weight? Whatever the shape or color, nobody likes afflictions! Another thing I've noticed, our moments don't seem to be the same as God's moments. It appears that God's moments last longer! Now I can go along with the idea that affliction is doing something more for me than just being there, and possibly in the end, things are going to work out fine. But that doesn't mean I want to get involved.

Thank God for verse 18! It says, "...while we do not look at the things which are seen, but at the things which are not seen. For the things which are seen are temporary, but the things which are not seen are eternal." We are encouraged by the apostle Paul not to focus our minds or attention on things that are temporary or fleeting. We are not to concentrate on things that will be here today and gone tomorrow. It's like placing all of your trust in the morning weather report. The forecast may say tomorrow will be partly cloudy with a 30 percent chance of rain, but then a west wind can come along and move the clouds eastward. Clouds may cover the sunshine, but covering doesn't negate the existence of the sun. All it takes is a strong wind to come along, and the clouds will move, revealing what has been hidden all along.

Circumstances are the same way; they are not a part of our world forever. They are temporary. They only last for a little while. Paul tells us that we are not to concentrate on them, not to be moved by them, not to keep our eyes glued to them, for they are not going to be with us always. On the other hand, we are told to keep our eyes on things that are eternal or that carry permanent weight.

The apostle Paul summarizes his thought when he says, "For we know that if our earthly house, this tent [that is, our physical body], is destroyed, we have a building from God, a house not made with hands, eternal in the heavens" (II Cor. 5:1).

In God's schematic, anything that dissolves precedes the existence of something greater. Therefore, we will not be left without a framework for the functioning of our faith—ever!

When I talk about this subject, I like to use the illustration of a bubble. How many of you remember blowing bubbles as children? Well, I do. (If you didn't blow bubbles, I'm sorry, you missed a whole lot of fun.) Imagine two bubbles side by side, close, but not quite touching. Let's call one bubble A and the other bubble B. Imagine that bubble A is faith and bubble B is also faith. As a matter of fact, let's have a little bit more fun with this. Add to A and B bubbles: C, D, E and F. (See Fig. 1.) In your mind, situate these bubbles on a very straight line. Now, let's go back to bubble A.

Consider bubble A to be the beginning of your life. All the world you know is in bubble A. You live in it, eat in it, and you breathe in it. Even your job or career is in bubble A. As a matter of fact, you do not even know of the existence of bubbles B, C, D, E, or F. Let's use your career as our example. As the years pass, your career begins to

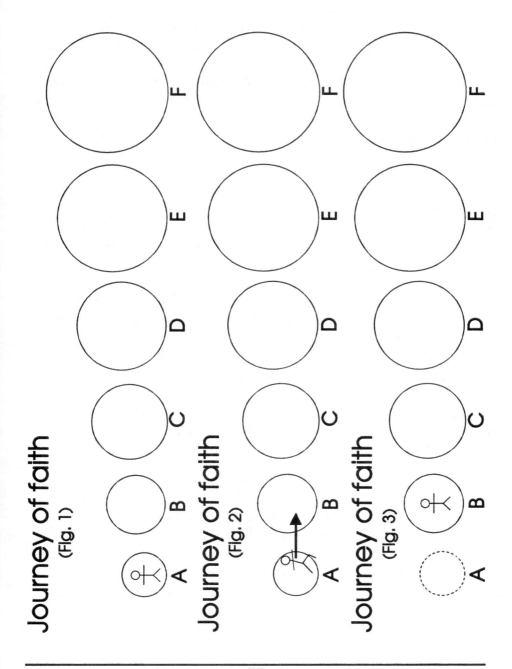

grow. Your mental capacity and abilities grow. You grow financially, and you grow spiritually. But after a while, you start feeling that you've outgrown certain things. What has happened is bubble A is now too small for you to live in. It has become cramped, and you feel frustrated. It is at this point you become aware of bubble B. Bubble B is similar to bubble A, but just a little larger. You've now grown so large in bubble A that you feel the tension and realize that bubble A is soon going to burst, leaving you in the atmosphere without protection. (See Fig. 2.) You know it's time to move on, so you take your first step. You take your right foot, step out of bubble A and place it within the confines of bubble B. You then do the same with your left foot. You are now in bubble B. You look back only to find that bubble A has burst. (See Fig. 3.) Looking around, you find yourself in an entirely new world, with new challenges, new opportunities and new ways in which to display your ability. Bubble B is much like bubble A. You don't know where to begin, you don't know where you will end, you don't even know whether you will get to the point that you'll outgrow bubble B as you outgrew bubble A. This illustrates Romans 1:17, "For in it the righteousness of God is revealed from faith to faith...." The meaning of this passage is "out of faith into faith."

Life is like a river. Many people see it as just one WAVE rather than as a continuous flow. We see it moving from puberty to adolescence, young adulthood, adulthood and on to old age. We always pinpoint, "Oh, she's old, she's a teenager, or she's young." Of course, it's true from our viewpoint, but life is more than that. God views life as a continuous flow. If we were to stand on the banks of a river, we could not pick a point and say, "This is where the river begins, or this is where it ends." We couldn't pinpoint where it rained on Wednesday or stopped on Thursday. Life is like the flow of a river.

Being a musician, I'm familiar with the classics. When I hear Beethoven's *Moonlight Sonata*, I am aware that the entire sonata is made up of various movements. We are more familiar with some movements than others, but one movement does not constitute a song. A dancer knows that each song contains a series of choreographed steps. When the audience sees the entire dance, some may focus on one movement, while others focus on another. Regardless of what they remember, one series of steps is not the entire dance. In church we sit and listen to sermons or inspiring speeches. There may be one thousand people there, but I guarantee you, one thousand people will come away with one thousand different thoughts. During a sermon, we are aware of everything that is said, but certain points stand out in our minds more than others. During a play, we are aware of every scene, yet some scenes or some actions will stand out in our memory more than others.

This is where we get hung up. We have a tendency to view God's ways as steps rather than one continuous motion. God is a God of motion. So it is with faith. Faith is not something that we have only for a moment or for one "movement." As someone once said, we move from one degree of grace to another degree of grace. We flow from one faith to another faith. Although we go from faith to faith, remember that both of them are called faith. It is one continual flow. It is a point of vital interest that when we move out of bubble A into bubble B, we find that bubble A is destroyed. The reason is to keep us from going back.

In the Bible, Moses stood on the banks of the Red Sea, stretched out his rod, and the waters parted (see

Ex. 14:13-28). The children of Israel crossed over on dry land. When the last person got to the other side, the Bible tells us, the waters closed up again. Why? Because once God's people moved into the next "bubble of faith," there was no going back to Egypt. Why couldn't they go back? Because God was not there. The previous "bubble" was shattered. There was nothing ahead of them but another glory or another step of faith. The just shall live from faith to faith. The Scripture says that the rightousness of God is revealed out of faith into faith, not out of faith into faith and back into the faith from which we came! The revelation of God comes as we continue to move in the flow of God.

In modern day so-called "movements" of God, we get hung up on the movements rather than see the entire flow. Someone in a wheelchair is healed, and we say, "God, do that for me." We see someone who has struck it rich in oil, and we say, "God, do that for me." I hear pastors and evangelists refer to testimonies of healings that took place 20 years ago, and it disturbs me, because I know that's what God did in that bubble of faith. But what is God doing today? Has he moved us to another faith? Is He moving us to another glory? We cannot afford to be stuck at movements such as the Welsh Revival or Azusa Street. We cannot afford to be stuck or trapped in the realm of the charismatic movement or live forever in a Word of Faith movement. Of course, I'm not talking about the scriptural word of faith, "...the word of faith which we preach..." (Rom. 10:8); I am talking about taking a biblical truth and camping around it. Each of these movements were "bubbles" of glory or "bubbles" of faith. Each movement was a seed planted in the ground and allowed to die, in order that it might give birth to the next place in God where our boats should be sailing. "For in Him we live and *move* and have our being..." (Acts 17:28, emphasis added).

If we could use a word to sum up all of this it would be *transitions*. Transitions can be viewed as some of the darkest times of our lives.

I once was the pastor of a church in a small town of eight thousand people. We had some pretty good times. God was faithful to us in every area. As a matter of fact, I started off with a salary of 75 dollars a week and a structurally unleveled parsonage. Sounds depressing, but at least we had a roof over our heads. Three and a half years later, I began to sense that it was time to leave and begin the next phase of work to which we believed God had called us. Those three and a half years were bubble A. We had outgrown it, and it was time to move on to bubble B. It was time to make the *transition.*

Transitions are often very difficult. You usually wonder whether you are even making the right decisions. The transition can be moving to a new city or looking for a new job. The transition can be changing careers even though you have been trained for four to five years in another area. The transition can be coming home and finding out that your spouse has delivered the divorce papers. The transition can be finding out that your child is on narcotics. A transition doesn't have to be that drastic, it can be having to take a bus because your car is in the shop. A transition can be a leak in your home or apartment which forces you to live with someone else for a period of time. Whatever transitions you experience, they can be uncomfortable and inconvenient. But remember, God will always have something available to house your faith.

Transitions can present the most challenging times of our lives. When Jesus was dying on Calvary, He cried out, "My God, My God, why have You forsaken Me?" (Matt. 27:46). Now we know God is everywhere. But as far as Jesus was concerned, He had been forsaken by His Father. Jesus was not forsaken, He was just in transition. That day it was a cross, but three days later the transition would give way to resurrection.

So in reality we do not lose our faith, we are either in a state of misunderstanding, growth or transition. Whatever the state in which we find ourselves, the ultimate destination is resurrection! Resurrection is not always easy to see, because it is future. Then again, that's what trusting God is all about.

4

Can I Ever Believe Again?

Give me a place to stand and I will move the earth.

Archimedes

Experience is the best teacher, or so it's been said. Now, of course, experience is a teacher, but is it really the best teacher?

The word *experience* is basically a composite of two words, *ex*, meaning "out of," and *experientia,* meaning "to try to put to the test." Another definition is "an actual living through something." Experiences are living through an ordeal or a series of events. Experiences in life can have either a positive or negative effect.

Imagine a young couple, unmarried and with no commitments. As a matter of fact, they've just met. They go on their first date, enjoy a romantic dinner and a movie.

They later decide to toy a little bit with sex. They've seen it on television. They have heard much about protection—condoms and things of that sort, but what could possibly happen? So, why not? Unfortunately, the young lady winds up pregnant. This was their first experience with sex, and she winds up pregnant.

As a pastor, I've spoken many times to young ladies who've said, "I really didn't mean to do it...I didn't plan on doing it...it was an accident, and on my first time, I got pregnant."

This young lady and young man now have had an experience. They can give you a good lesson on what happens with a young life when you have sex and wind up pregnant. But that experience was unnecessary. It taught them something, but the lesson cost many years of their lives. It probably even altered the course of their lives.

So it is with God's Word. Experience can never be the validation of it. I grew up in a church where experience was everything. If you shouted (an emotional outburst in church), then you felt God. If you gave a good testimony, people would comment, "That person really knows God." If the choir belted out a riveting song, and you gave a visible show of emotion, that was considered to be an encounter with God. Experience often took the place of an inward truth.

However, our view of God's Word or how we live out the gospel is not to be based on our experiences. The reality of God's Word is based on what God plainly says. It is at this point that the greatest confrontation to our faith arises. That confrontation is *experience versus God's Word.*

I remember when I was very young, an elderly woman stood up one Sunday in the congregation, leaned on her cane and cried out, "I wouldn't have a 'ligion [religion] I couldn't feel sometimes." Now, I understood it, and I'm quite sure she did, too. But what happens when we can't "feel it?" What happens when God doesn't feel close? What happens when our moods shift or our emotions change? Suppose you wake up one morning and just don't feel like praying, you don't feel like meditating, or you don't feel like reading your Bible? This is that crucial point where confrontation arises between God's Word and our experiences. Experience is based on fact as we perceive it, but God's Word is based on God Himself. The Bible plainly tells us that God will never leave us or forsake us. Yet, there will be times when we experience the feeling of loneliness.

A few years ago, a young woman was brutally murdered in her apartment. She was a strong believer, a good church member, a tither and very serious about her relationship with the Lord. Yet, she was murdered. Saundra and I talked about this event over and over, as we often do. We're buffers for one another. We find that talking through situations somehow helps us find God even in the midst of tragedy and pain. The conversations go something like this:

"Edward, what happened?" Saundra asked.

"I really don't know," I replied.

Inwardly, I thought, *Here we have a young lady who has tried to do her best for God, and in the middle of the night we get a call saying she's been brutally killed. I* searched for God. I searched for answers, and yet I could not get a handle on it.

Saundra continued, "Why is it that people who do not believe in God or even acknowledge God seem to live lives that are trouble free, while on the other hand, good people, people who make mistakes, but basically are trying to do some good solid things within their church and within their community, wind up in tragedy?"

I concluded, "Well, that's something we can't answer. Maybe there was a problem, or maybe she did something wrong? We could speculate on a lot of those things, but in reality, we just don't know."

Here we have an experience, yet God promises to protect us. We've read in the Scripture portion we call the Lord's Prayer, "deliver us from evil." Why was she not delivered from evil? Isn't murder evil? Where was her protection? We teach about angels watching over us and angels protecting us, so where were her angels? Where was her protection? This was something that happened which seems to be contrary to God's Word.

The Bible says, "Surely He shall deliver you from the snare of the fowler and from the perilous pestilence" (Ps. 91:3). Why is it that Christians are contracting AIDS through blood transfusions? Is this their fault? The Bible also says, "A thousand may fall at your side, and ten thousand at your right hand; but it shall not come near you" (Ps. 91:7). But every day, people who are good, strong, solid Christians are dying. The Scriptures read, "No evil shall befall you, nor shall any plague come near your dwelling...Because he has set his love upon Me, therefore I will deliver him..." (Ps. 91:10,14). Does this mean that God does not love us if we are not delivered? Is this a sign that we have somehow fallen from grace? This Scripture goes on to say, "...I will set him on high, because he has known My name" (Ps. 91:14). Does this mean I do not know the name or the character of God because my life is at a low moment? "He shall call upon Me, and I will answer him..." (Ps. 91:15). I'm quite sure that in tragic situations we call upon the name of God. Is it that God couldn't hear or that He didn't really listen? "With long life I will satisfy him, and show him My salvation" (Ps. 91:16). Why is a young life snuffed out so quickly?

These experiences seem to contradict God's Word. These passages carry the promise to deliver us, yet we find instances in the Bible that seem to contradict these words.

What about the story of Cain and Abel? Abel did what God said. Abel paid his tithes. Abel worshiped God. Abel believed the God of his father, Adam, while Cain, on the other hand, was basically self-serving. Cain did what he wanted to do, and when it came down to worshiping God with his offering, Cain withheld the best and gave God the leftovers. If anyone should have gotten the shaft, it should have been Cain. Yet Cain murdered Abel. Why did God allow it?

Jeremiah and Isaiah, mighty prophets of God, were murdered. The apostles of Jesus died martyrs' deaths; they were stoned, crucified, run through by stakes. And what about John the Baptist, the cousin of Jesus Himself? John stood up against Herod concerning a social evil, and for standing up against Herod, it was at the whim of

Herodias' daughter that John's head was cut off. John was murdered, and Jesus didn't even stop it! Yet, the Bible talks about protection.

Now here's a good one for you—Jesus Christ Himself. I know the Bible tells us that Jesus said no man could take His life, but He would give His life, and we know that Jesus gave His life for the salvation of the world. But the fact remains, from a natural point of view, Jesus was crucified on a cruel device called the cross. This was murder. Yet according to God's Word, He will deliver those who call upon His name. If God's Word is truth, then why does experience seem to contradict His promises?

We can apply natural reasoning and say, "Well, maybe there is hidden sin...maybe this individual was doing something behind closed doors of which we are not aware." I've had people come to me and say, "The reason you ran out of gas on the highway... "or "the reason you were evicted from your apartment, is because God is getting back at you for something bad you did." But what about an innocent baby who has not even had a chance to learn the English language? What about a toddler who has just learned to walk? Even Jesus, who was said not to have known sin, experienced the cross.

None of this seems fair, but we react to hurtful and devastating situations according to our system of belief. The definition of the word *system* is a "set or arrangement of things so related or connected as to form a unit or organic whole." Everybody has a belief system. We have a set of truths that are intertwined one with another.

For the sake of example, let's say I believe that the sun is hot. I believe that if you lie in the sun with your skin exposed, it will burn you. Now because of that belief, I do not go out into the sun with my skin exposed for long periods of time.

Centuries ago, it was believed that the world was flat. Therefore, many explorers or would-be explorers would only go so far in their ships. When one explorer finally changed his system of belief, believing that the world was round, he went beyond what the other explorers had done and sailed around the world. Why did he sail around the world while other explorers limited their sailing? Was it because their ships were different? No, it was because of a system of belief.

Every single one of us has a system of belief. Whether we are Christians, Muslims, Hindus or Jews, regardless of our denomination or background, we all have a system of belief. We view the world, the circumstances and situations of life, through the microscope of the belief system. We come to conclusions about life, morals and society based upon our system of belief. The treacherous institution of slavery that was forced upon an entire race of people was fueled by a system of belief.

Consequently, what we believe dictates how we react to the things around us. How we believe is always tied together with how we react to situations, tragic or otherwise.

In some circles of thought, individuals will accept any and every event as the will of God. If someone is killed in an auto accident they'll say, "Well, it must have been the will of God." If someone is murdered they will say, "It must have been the will of God." It stands to reason that if it was the will of God, then God was involved. Some people find comfort in that system of belief. They can't explain it, so they conclude that it must be the will of God.

In other circles of thought, hurt, sickness, disease and tragedy are seen as normal happenings in life. These people say, "Well, that's just the way the cookie crumbles...it's just a throw of the dice...you're either lucky or unlucky."

Others take the Word of God, read it and apply it without scholarship or thought as to historical context. They see in Scripture that God will deliver us; God will take care of us. These persons often are upbeat and positive, until a tragedy happens within their family or to someone close. Then they cannot reconcile God's Word with their experience. Of course, something happens to their system of belief; it breaks down because of apparent contradictions to their understanding of God's Word. This naturally leads to a shattered faith in God. Our system of belief is like a tapestry of interwoven accepted truths. When that tapestry is ripped, we must struggle to believe again. Somewhere down the line, there are going to be things in life for which there are no explanations, that is, no explanations we can presently comprehend.

The apostle Paul wrote, "For what if some did not believe? Will their unbelief make the faithfulness of God without effect?" (Rom. 3:3). In other words, if we don't believe something, it does not change its validity. What we believe or do not believe does not shift God's standards any higher or lower.

We tend to view life only from our own frame of reference. We see events around us in the context of their natural settings. But we are part of more than one dimension.

Of course, we live on a natural plane or in a realm of touchable things. God created mankind with physical sensors. We have the ability to see, hear, touch, smell and taste. This is how man relates to the natural world. However, God not only gave man the physical ability to relate to his world, but He gave him a spirit. The spirit of man enables him to touch another world, the world of God. "Now faith is the substance of things hoped for, the evidence of things not seen" (Heb. 11:1).

If faith is the substance of things hoped for, then faith is something that can be touched. We may not be able to touch it through our physical senses, yet it can be touched. Faith is touched through another world or another dimension. In light of this, we can conclude that experiences upon this earth and experiences in God's dimension are happening simultaneously.

Once after leaving a convention in Washington, D.C., a friend and I drove night and day in order to get back to Houston. A very small dinner had been planned in honor of my birthday. When we got to Houston, instead of going to my home, we drove to our church facilities. The excuse was that my friend had to pick up a package. I thought nothing of it. When I got to the church, I walked up the stairs as I normally did, and all the lights were out. When I turned the lights on, a multitude of people yelled, "Surprise!" and they threw confetti all over the place. Now, I had been in Washington unaware of the events being planned in Houston. Two things had been happening on two different levels, and my ignorance of one level did not stop the plans.

It's the same with the God of the universe. God is involved with a plan. On our plane, we may not know anything about it, but it does not mean the plan does not exist, nor does it mean that it will not overlap our world. Therefore, our experiences cannot be the validation of God's Word.

At this point, you may say, "This all sounds great, but the bottom line is that I hurt, and oh, God, how it hurts! Theory, philosophy and theology are good, but they are not helping me very much at this point. My husband has just walked out the door and left me with three children to raise. Now an extra paycheck is gone." Or maybe you've just discovered that a sister or brother has been diagnosed with cancer. Maybe you're the pastor of a church that's behind on the rent, and they're threatening to put a padlock on the door. Maybe you're one who is pregnant without a husband, or you've just heard that your life is on the verge of termination through AIDS. At this point, theory does not help. Why? Because your entire system of belief has been shattered.

You have been taught to believe in a good God. A God who hears and answers prayer. You've prayed, you've believed, you've fasted, you've done everything that you know to do, but still sickness is in your body. Your emotions still are going haywire. At this particular point in time you don't need theory, you need to repair the belief system.

The stability of what we believe is supported by our view of God's Word and not our experiences. This is where solid Christianity comes into play. Do we believe what God has actually said, or do we believe what we have chosen to believe God has said?

We've all heard the statement, "the truth hurts." In all honesty, truth does not hurt. Truth is not like a gun or knife which can inflict pain. But when our perception of certain principles is shattered by the reality of God's Word, we can become disoriented.

Every now and then, someone I haven't seen for a long time will approach me after a worship service and I'll ask, "Where have you been?" The reply will go something like this:

"Well, I've been having a hard time. I lost my job about three months ago. I knew I was a tither, a good supporter of my church, a decent father and husband, yet I was laid off. Why?"

"So, why haven't you been to church?" I'd ask.

"Well, I just didn't feel like hearing God stuff! It didn't seem to work when I needed it."

What you have here is a person who has had his entire system of belief shattered and is now disoriented. Psalm 23 says, "Yea, though I walk through the valley of the shadow of death...." The psalmist was experiencing disorientation. He knew that it didn't feel very good, but he wasn't quite sure what the outcome would be. Thank God his belief system was intact, for he said, "...I will fear no evil; for You are with me."

When our system of belief is shattered, we lose our reference points. Every Scripture we have been taught to believe just doesn't seem to hold water at this point. We're not sure whether we are coming or going. We're like ships without a compass. It's like driving to a destination without a map, unsure of whether you're going east or west.

In Chapter 2, I told the story of driving my family to the mountains of Colorado after my daughter went to be with the Lord. When I finally reached the top of a high mountain, I knelt down in the snow to somehow pray. I was devastated and tears were gushing every 15 or 20 seconds. I wanted to feel God's presence or some emotional peace. I wanted to hear a voice that would say everything would be alright. But I didn't hear it. I felt nothing. I was disoriented. I began to question who I was, what I was preaching, what I believed. Thoughts flooded my mind, *It's all been a farce, it doesn't mean anything... What are you going to say to people when you return?...Can you ever trust God again...?*

I now look back on that experience realizing that what I believed concerning God's Word was in direct conflict with my experience.

However, when experience and God's Word seemingly conflict, we must understand that *God's Word is not proven by our experiences.* I'm quite sure there are some who will debate me on that point. It might be said, "I believed that God was a healer, and I was healed. Therefore, He is a healer." Believe me I don't argue with that. Some may say, "I did not have enough money to pay my rent. I prayed and asked God for the money, and just before the rent was due, God gave me the money." I've experienced that in my own life, too many times. But these experiences are ones in which the outcome was positive. What about the ones who prayed for God to pay the rent, yet when the rent became due, the money was not there? That individual could say, based on experience that God did not keep His Word.

My point is that neither of these experiences can be used as indicators of God's faithfulness. God's faithfulness is based on what His Word says—and His Word *only*! Our experiences will vary. Our feelings will change. But God's Word remains the same, whether our experiences concur or run contrary.

A biblical passage says, "Forever, O Lord, Your Word is settled in Heaven" (Ps. 119:89). God's Word becomes our place to stand. Regardless of our feelings or our experiences, God's Word is settled. In other words, there is no sinking ground. It's done. Regardless of our experiences, His Word is "set in concrete."

God's Word does not need our experiences to validate it. God's Word is what it is. Someone else's healing cannot be the basis for our healing. God's Word is that basis! What we believe must be based solely on what God says and not on the experience of someone else.

So what do we do? Ignore testimonies? Of course not! God forbid! I love testimonies. I rejoice when I hear people talk of near-accidents in which the car miraculously swerved. I rejoice to hear people tell of near-fatal tragedy or of going to a doctor with a tumor, only to leave the office with the doctor wondering where it went! These are miracles. Miracles are the interventions of God in the natural course of events. But miracles cannot be the basis on which to fix our lives. Our lives must be fixed upon God's Word and God's Word alone—regardless of experiences. Testimonies are not designed to build one's faith to the level of receiving what someone else has received.

A preacher will stand and say, "...just as John was healed, you can be healed also...," and sure enough, every time, someone in that audience will come to the front and say, "Pray for me...I want to be healed just like John." But John's experience is *his* experience with God. There are two dimensions involved: John's dimension and God's dimension. When we go to God, we cannot go to God saying, "God, do for me what you did for John." We must discover what God is saying to us about us. We cannot place our hopes and trust in what John received, rather it must be in what God says to us.

Testimonies are designed to draw us into God's world. Testimonies excite us. Testimonies encourage us. Testimonies tell us that all things are possible. They cause our faith to soar. They cause our hopes to build. Testimonies encourage us to stretch beyond ourselves. But the goal is not to receive what someone else received. Your goal is to acquire absolute trust in God.

To be very honest with you, whether we are healed instantly or later is not the issue. The issue is not whether our rent is paid later or on time or whether your estranged spouse comes back home or never returns. The issue is what does God's Word say?

The goal is to dig deeper into Him. *Yes, God, it hurts. Yes, God, my world has been shattered. Yes, God, my experience was tragic. Yes, God, my system of belief has been torn to shreds. But the regaining of a place to stand is now possible because of Your Word.*

You can believe again because the foundation of your belief is not in the shifting winds of experience, but on the solid rock of God's Word. It would take a change in God for God's Word to change. And my friends, that just won't happen because God has already committed Himself by saying, "I change not!"

Oh, God, I hurt. But I also recognize that You are the Healer of hurts. No longer do I trust in my experiences alone. I place my trust in Your Word. God, give me a hunger for Your Word. Let me taste and see that You are good. I now find my place to stand. Not in my experience, but in Your unchangeable Word. Amen.

5

If Only You Could Understand

The power of perception is that which we call the understanding....The soul begins to have ideas when it begins to perceive.

John Locke

Many circumstances in life make us uncomfortable. That's nothing new. We've handled them before, and most likely we'll handle them again. But what really gets to us is not understanding why they happen.

Let's take Al and Mary for instance. Al had come in from a rough day at work. It was Friday evening, and all day everything had seemed to go wrong for Al. He was tired, so he sprawled across the bed and got a half hour of sleep. Later he got up, took a shower and headed for the dinner table. When he got there, he noticed that the children were unusually quiet. What he didn't know was that little Al had received two D's on his report card, and Elizabeth had had to stay after school for copying another girl's homework. Al's wife, Mary, was explaining all of this while Al was trying to eat, but Al was not paying much attention. He was in a different world.

After dinner Al slumped into his favorite old chair, turned on the TV and entered the world of network fantasy. Al downed two or three beers and fell asleep, as he normally did, anticipating a Saturday of TV sports with no interruptions.

Before Al knew it, it was Saturday night. As he prepared to go to sleep, Mary asked,

"Al, are you going to church with me and the kids in the morning?"

Al replied, "Aw, Mary, do I have to?"

"Well, of course not, but I think that every once in a while it would be good for the children to see their father in church."

"Mary, I think I know what's best for our kids. I work hard all week long. I had a really tough time this week, and it's going to take the weekend just for me to recuperate. After all, my God-given task is to provide for this home, and I'm doing the best I can. I don't believe two hours on Sunday is going to make a difference one way or the other. I can pray at home as well as I can anywhere else."

Mary, weary of hearing the same argument week after week, year after year, responded, "Al, I've been going to church with the children for years.

They're growing up. They're having problems in school, and they need direction. They need spiritual direction, and Al, I...uh...don't mean to be pushy, but some of it has to come from you. I believe if you took the time...."

"Now there you go again, Mary, always coming down on me for not taking time with the kids. It's always about church. Church! Church! I'm tired of hearing about that church! Can't we ever talk about anything else? And another thing, if you would spend more time at home with me, maybe our relationship would be a little better. When I really want and need you, you're always at that church. I'm getting fed up with it."

Mary snaps back, "Al, what's the problem? Why are you so anti-church? I've seen you. You sneak in the living room late at night, get on your knees and pray. I've watched you walk around the backyard, looking up into the sky and moving your lips. I know you believe in God. So what's the problem? I think...."

Al interrupts, "Mary, you don't understand. I've had some bad experiences in the past, and I don't intend for those things to happen again. That's the problem with us. You just don't understand."

"I'm not stupid," Mary said. "What do you mean, I don't understand?"

"Just what I said. You don't understand. You've never understood!"

Mary began to cry. Al knew he was getting to her.

"There you go again, always crying. Every time I try to explain myself you start crying."

"But Al, that's the problem. You're not explaining—you're hollering! I'm tired of always being hollered at."

"Hollering, *hollering, me*? Who's hollering? I'm just tired of you always butting into my business. Stay out of my life. You just don't understand!"

Sound familiar? Well it should, because it happens in millions of homes, every day, all across America.

People want to be understood. But the reality in life is that we are seldom understood. People cannot read minds, consequently, our best intentions and greatest humane acts can go unnoticed.

****

"It's the biggest scam to hit Cleveland, Ohio, since 1973," the DA thundered.

"I object," countered the defense attorney, "it has not been proven that my client has taken one dime!"

"Objection overruled," the judge replied without emotion.

Rev. James was the last one you would expect to get involved in crooked dealings. It all had started with a chain letter that promised a hundred percent return on the reader's money. Rev. James needed money for his project to house the homeless. He followed the procedure necessary to continue the chain letter and mailed it to ten of the top contributors on his mailing list. They sent money by return mail, but it didn't return to Rev. James. Somehow the money got into the wrong hands.

For 25 years Rev. James had fed the hungry, housed the homeless and reigned as champion of the poor and needy within the city. He had 25 years of active ministry filled with honesty and integrity, but now 25 years of ministry were going down the drain, all because of one chain letter. No one wanted to associate with Rev. James. No one wanted even to admit that they knew him.

People love "tea!" I'm not talking about the beverage, I'm referring to an American slang phrase, *pouring tea,* which is taken from the habit of individuals sitting around a table drinking tea while gossiping about others.

Everything that is done in the dark shall come to light— TV lights that is! Everywhere we look, someone is being accused of something—adultery, corruption, mismanagement of funds or selling of junk bonds. It really doesn't matter what it is, because these things boost media ratings. They sell newspapers. You'll find it in the courtroom, the boardroom, the White House or the church house. The question comes to mind, "Is there nothing sacred?"

All of us at one time or another have been accused of something. It doesn't have to be a multimillion-dollar scandal. It can be taking someone's ink pen from their desk without thinking. It can be a husband questioning his wife concerning her whereabouts for the past two hours. It doesn't matter how great or small the accusation is, it doesn't feel very good to be accused, especially if you're not able to explain your position or get your point across. Unfortunately, there are thousands of people who spend a lifetime trying to prove their innocence, and rarely do they succeed. If they do, they seldom regain the status or respect among their peers that they once had.

Our country has been saturated with courtroom antics and congressional fiascoes. We are a people who thrive on the spectacular. But what we fail to realize is that in every situation or accusation, somebody gets hurt. Somebody feels the pain of exposure or the gut-wrenching feeling of being misunderstood. Yes, it hurts not to be understood.

We place ourselves in the position to be hurt, because we believe we can correct every misunderstanding. The fact is everyone will not understand you, and you will not understand everything.

Jesus lived with misunderstandings. He was misunderstood by just about everybody around Him. He was misunderstood by the religious leaders of His time, misunderstood by the community leaders and misunderstood by those in the political system. They misunderstood His mission, His purpose, His plans and even His teaching. The very reason He came was misunderstood by those who walked with Him every day. If we had walked in the shoes of Jesus, we probably would have appealed to the Supreme Court of that time period in order to "save our ministry" or "clear our name."

Jesus did not waste His time trying to explain everything. Even from the cross, when spectators mocked, "...If He is the King of Israel, let Him now come down from the cross, and we will believe Him..." (Matt. 27:42), Jesus remained silent. He even commented in prayer while dying, "Father forgive them—they just don't understand" (Ed's paraphrase of Luke 23:34).

Here we find a significant key for living: The fact that we are misunderstood should not be taken personally or internalized. We can live with misunderstanding, but it cannot be allowed to live inside us.

Jesus lived with being misunderstood, but He never allowed it to stop Him from fulfilling His mission. Being misunderstood had nothing to do with Calvary; it had nothing to do with what Jesus had to defeat through the cross. People did not understand His mission; however, this had nothing to do with the plan of God concerning the Resurrection. So it must be with us. We will never fulfill our purpose in life as long as we allow misunderstanding by people to get inside us. It will rob us of our drive, our motivation and our ability to overcome obstacles.

If we would take the time to admit it, there are things that we do not understand concerning the Word of God. But that does not exempt us from doing what God says. We may not understand why we should tithe, but we must because God says to do it. We may not understand why it is necessary for us to forgive, but we must because God says to do it.

We live in a world where people will not always grasp what our personal lives are all about, but that's the way life is. Our purpose is not to be liked, but to fulfill what God has for us to do. It is possible to be acquainted with a multiplicity of individuals, yet not always understand everyone. But we were not commanded to understand one another, we were commanded to love one another.

I travel in a wide variety of "religious" circles. I meet a lot of good Christian people. I also meet seekers, those whom Jesus characterized as being not far from the Kingdom. A few years ago, I had the privilege of being involved in a very interesting discussion.

From birth Ray had been raised in a fundamentalist church (whatever fundamentalist is). His understanding of religion was unequaled. Thomas, on the other hand, had attended a very liberal school in the East. His main concern was solving the social ills of his generation. Next came John. John believed that unless you speak in tongues, you could not possibly have an encounter with God. I, personally, hadn't formed any particular doctrines. I just loved people (and to tell you the truth, after what I'm about to tell you happened between Ray, John, Thomas and me, I wonder whether I even did that very well!)

Now I opened the conversation about a movie I had seen. (Why did I ever bring that up?) Ray was the first to comment.

"Brother, I believe every man has the right to live his own life, but do you frequent movies often?"

"If I hear it's a good one, I go every time I get a chance," I replied.

Ray mumbled, "Well, uh...that seems to be a poor witness for the cause...."

Thomas interrupted, "Ray, what's wrong with the movies? That's the problem. We are afraid to go where the people are."

John uneasily commented, "I've seen some of the movies they make today, but I usually walk out halfway through, especially if what's on the screen grieves the Holy Spirit."

Thomas being somewhat frustrated at their comments said, "That's the problem with you fundamentalists and holy roller people, you're so afraid of...."

"Afraid of what?" John replied. "I'm not afraid of anything! I just don't give any place to the devil!"

"That's right," Ray added. "If Jesus were to come and catch you in a movie theater, you would go straight to hell...."

"Well, I wouldn't go as far as to say all of that," John said. "You know, greater is He that is in us than he that...."

"There you go again, quoting all of those Scriptures, John," Ray snapped. "After all, that's where the people are, and we've been commissioned to go where the people are."

Thomas raised his eyebrows, as he always does when he's about to speak.

"I know what you are about to say, Thomas," Ray said sarcastically.

"Well, what's wrong with that?" Thomas replied. "You have something against reaching people? What about the drug addict? The homeless? The ones discriminated against racially?"

"Thomas, what does homelessness have to do with this discussion? We are talking about movies."

Ray was becoming irritated with what he considered Thomas' shallowness.

"All I know is that all of you need to be filled with the Holy Ghost and fire! Ah-ba-ba-ba....!" John turned back to the book he was reading with a gesture he always used when he thought himself to be right.

Simultaneously, Ray and Thomas chorused, "What do you mean by that? Are you implying that we don't have the Holy Ghost?"

"Well, neither of you speak in tongues."

After that statement, John leaned on the two back legs of his chair and began to rock back and forth smugly.

"Tongues?" Thomas shouted. "Tongues?"

"Let me tell you one thing." Ray had just about as much as he could take of John's self-righteousness.

It was at this point that I wished I had never brought up the subject of movies. The ironic part about it was that the movie was Walt Disney's *101 Dalmatians*, rated G.

I learned a very valuable lesson that day. I learned to keep my mouth shut! I learned that whenever I'm around people of various persuasions, I should talk only about the weather! Even that might be a mistake—John probably would want to make a spiritual Word confession and drive away the rain! Since that conversation, I have come to a concussion—oh, I mean conclusion, excuse me!

Our understanding is constructed from birth with intellectual building blocks. Psychologists of our time can do a far better job of explaining this than I can. But I do know that the shape and consistency of those building blocks are affected by the environment in which we grow up, secular or religous.

No wonder God allows the shattering of our feeble attempts to understand the mysteries of the universe. Is it because He doesn't want us to know them? Of course not. He allows them to be shattered piece by piece, moment by moment, day by day, from glory to glory, in order to reorganize them. His new structure will allow us to gain greater insight into Himself.

Centuries ago, a fellow by the name of Job had the same problem. One day, as the poor guy woke up, somebody came running through the door, shook him and said, "Wake up, Job, hurry, get your clothes on. Fire just fell from the sky and wiped out all of your cattle." Job probably sat back and said, "Oh, my goodness, what else could possibly happen?" Before the servant could even get it out of his mouth, another servant stumbled through the door saying, "Sir, a few of the workers were outside plowing up the field, and a group of men came along and slaughtered them with swords." Job asked, "All of them?" "Yes, Job, all of them."

About this time Job was getting a little "teed off!" While he was questioning that servant, another came in, "I wanted to let you know that a group of people from the other side of town came by. They were talking about how tired they were of you being the richest man around, so they formed about three gangs, raided the fields and took the livestock, and by the way, they also killed the foreman with a sword. I'm the only one left to tell you about it. I think they left me alive to bring the message."

Before Job could even open his mouth, the final serv-ant ran in and said, "Job, all of your children were in one house, and suddenly a great wind came across the desert and caved in the walls. All of the chilren are dead."

After all of this, the only thing Job could do was fall on his face and worship God. Why? I really don't know. The natural thing to do would be to curse God. Job probably wondered, "Can it get any worse?" Well, Job old boy, it can.

Days later, Job developed a terrible disease, a type of leprosy that brought him near death. He had lost his money, his children and even his health. His wife later said to him, in so many words, that God didn't seem very friendly toward him. "Why don't you go ahead and give Him a piece of your mind, curse Him, die, and be through with it?" But for some reason, Job decided to trust God.

During his ordeal, some friends came by the house. Job thought maybe they would be able to give him some insight. The conversations were a total disaster! I mean everybody had a reason for Job's problem—either he had sinned, didn't pray enough or didn't have enough faith. They had more reasons for his predicament than roaches in Houston!

It's not that much different today. Whenever tragic things, or things we don't understand, happen in life, we have a tendency to find a nice little neatly packaged answer that will substantiate our belief. It disturbs us when we don't have answers. It disturbs us when we can-not package the answers and hide them in the attic of our memories, so as to not deal with them again. This was the mission of Job's friends, to help him tie up his problems in a lot of neat, orderly boxes.

But finally, God just would not hold His thoughts in any longer, and for several chapters in the book of Job, God questioned the understanding of Job.

So what was the conclusion? God confronted Job with his own intellectual inadequacies, to the extent that all Job could do was hide his face, admit his inadequacies and hope to go on with life from there.

Of course, Job faced a tragic situation, but there was some humor. Every time Job would say, "Oh, God, You are so right; hallelujah, praise You Lord; I bow my face before You and...," God would say, "Quiet, Job, I'm not finished yet." God would go on for another chapter. Finally, when he thought God was through, Job replied, "God, You are something else. I never realized how powerful...." "Shut up, Job," God would reply, "I'm not finished yet." Finally after God had finished, I firmly believe there was a space of quietness. Job did not want to be rebuked by God again! Eventually, Job replied, "God, I've heard about You, but now I see You with my own eyes. I'm aware of You in a way that I've never been aware of You before."

When we experience things in our lives that we don't understand, God somehow reminds us that even in the midst of our misunderstanding, He is still God. We come to that place where we experience God in another dimension. We come to know a God who is beyond sermons, songs and Sunday school lessons. We become aware of Him in a way or dimension that we have never known before. Come to think of it, I believe God gets a kick out of shattering our shallow sanctuaries of understanding. Yet, whatever God shatters, God replaces.

God never leaves us without a vehicle through which our faith can operate. God never consigns us to a challenge for which we will not have the strength. He never leaves us in a situation that we do not have the intellect and power to overcome. God never leaves us in the midst of a doubt that does not have a door which leads to faith. Whenever there is a need, always know that God has supplied an answer. We may not see the answer, but it's there.

According to Scripture, Abraham's wife, Sarah, had asked that her bondwoman, Hagar, be thrown out of the camp along with her son, Ishmael. (Ishmael was Abraham's son by Hagar, but Sarah's son, Isaac, one day was to inherit his father's position. Sarah didn't want problems from Hagar.) The account tells us that Hagar wandered in the desert with the child. The child was about to die of thirst, so she prayed to God for help. God opened her eyes, and she saw a well of water. It does not say that God created a well of water miraculously. It says that God opened her eyes, and there it was. There are answers all around us. All around are God's ways of meeting our needs. We may not see them at the moment, but as we continue to trust Him, they eventually come into focus.

Why do some babies die at birth while others live? I honestly don't understand. Why do good people have bad things happen to them, and bad people seem to get off scot-free? Who knows? Why does it seem that irreverent people seem to "get away with murder?" Why do the rich ignore God and get richer, while the poor pray harder and get poorer? Why do church-going people seem to get the wrong end of the stick? Why does it seem always to rain on a Sunday when the Pastor preaches his best sermon and only the faithful attend? To these and other questions we really don't have an answer. Our understanding is limited. But then again, would knowing why change the outcome? Probably not. Maybe knowing why is not enough. Maybe all we need is the knowledge that God understands. Maybe, just maybe, having faith that God knows is more than enough to get us through.

Oh, God, teach me to trust Your ways, for Your thoughts are higher than mine. I am growing each day in Your ways and Your thinking. But until that time when I fully understand, I will rest in the comfort that You know Your job. Amen.

6

God-in-the-Box

When sinful man makes reason his primary
source of knowing God, he idolatrously creates
God in his own image, he creates the God that he
wants to worship. Reason forms its systems, sets
its standards, and then demands that God fit the
standards that it has erected.

William Hordern

"All around the cobbler's bench, the monkey chased the
weasel. Da, da, da, da, da, da, da, da—pop goes the
weasel!" I forget the words, but I never forget the tune. Do
you remember that special little toy called a jack-in-the-
box? It was nothing more than a tin box with a crank
handle on the side. As you turned it, the music would play
and a small clown would pop out. Of course, his name
was Jack. But the amazing thing was that Jack always
popped out at a certain point during the familiar tune. So
what does this have to do with anything spiritual? Plenty.

A man named John was struggling to keep his construction business from finally going under. John was very aggressive and had pulled himself up by his own bootstraps. After he had begun his work in corporate America, he moved up the ladder very swiftly. He was one of very few men able to handle three regions at a time. John was the epitome of what most consider successful. He owned a Mercedes, dressed in the latest fashions and owned a house nestled in the suburbs. John was a very outgoing and cheerful fellow and never allowed anything to stop him. But somewhere down the line his business took a turn for the worse. John was three notes behind on his Mercedes and house. He had even become a little leery about contacting his clients; it seems his assurance was a bit shaky. So one day John came to my office.

> "Pastor, I don't understand. I've done all I know to do, and my business hasn't turned around. What do I do?"

> I had to do some probing, so I asked, "Have you been meditating on the Word of God?"

> "Yes, every morning."

John was searching my facial expressions for some sign that would tell him he had nothing to worry about.

> "Are you managing your money?" I asked.

> "To the best of my ability," he replied.

> "How's the morale among your employees? Are you listening to them? Are you upgrading their working conditions on a consistent basis?"

"Yes! Yes! Yes! I'm doing all of that!"

I could see the frustration in his eyes. I had always known John to be honest and straightforward. He wasn't a complainer. He'd had rough times before, but this was different. I knew he needed some answers.

Finally I asked, "So what do you make of this puzzle?"

John thought for a moment, his eyes aimed at the carpet. Then slowly looking up, he gazed, stopping to peer through the window behind me.

"Pastor, I don't understand it. I've gone straight down the line—prayer, fasting, confession, meditation, action and the other things you've taught me. I've received insight from countless books and tapes. I know every evangelist, every pastor, even every talk show host who appears on television. I know their messages by heart. I've got stacks of return envelopes for contributions on my desk, and I've even sent money to some. But no matter how I try, I just can't seem to get this thing working."

I knew what John felt, but I didn't have any answers. I had no formulas. It's interesting how pastors feel that whenever someone walks into their office, by the time they walk out, all of the questions should be answered or every problem solved. But in this case, I felt hopeless. Here was a man that I had known for years. His business was going down the drain, and there was nothing I could do or say to stop it.

Occasionally, I would stare up at the ceiling as if to get an answer from some great power. But nothing was coming. Evidently, it wasn't a time for answers, but a time for compassion. It was a time for comfort. I should have cried with him, but interestingly enough, all I could offer was a prayer, a squeeze of the hand and a nod of understanding, or at least a nod of wishing I could understand. But before I realized what I was about to say, I had said it.

"God is not a jack-in-the-box."

John slowly raised his head, arched his right eyebrow and quizzed, "What was that you said, Pastor?"

I said, "God is not a jack-in-the-box."

How many times have we sought to squeeze God into the "box" of our doctrines, place the box on a certain shelf and, when trouble comes, go to that exact spot on the shelf and look for God? We play the tune of our spiritual formulas, right down the line, one, two, three, four; and just as with the jack-in-the-box tune, we think we know when to expect God to pop out. When He doesn't, our faith is shattered.

God doesn't always pop out on time! (Nothing new, huh?) God doesn't always answer at the "right" moment. There will be times when, no matter what we do, we won't be able to persuade God to do it like He did it before.

I took my time and spoke to John with one ear on his problem and another tuned to Heaven. I continued the discourse and said, "John, it is here that we must exercise patience. Patience is one of the most difficult concepts to be grasped by American believers. Patience is the ability to endure, it's the ability to stand still even though a storm is swiftly approaching. Patience is the ability to trust God even when we feel untrusting."

John left my office that day with probably no more insight than when he had come in. Then on the other hand, maybe he did. I've learned through the years that we will not always have the exact answer that people want us to have. We will not always know for sure that we have given the correct formula.

In the Book of Esther, Mordecai said to Esther, "Yet who knows whether you have come to the kingdom for such a time as this?" (Esther 4:14). The phrase that sticks in situations like this is "who knows...?" "Who knows" may seem to some to be a statement indicating confusion, but it's not.

Early one autumn morning in Virginia Beach, I was scheduled to co-host *The 700 Club* when I noticed the sky from my hotel window at about 6:45 a.m. It was that time when night was still visible in the west, yet the dawn had begun in the east. The question arose, "Where does night end and day begin?" As I tried to figure it out, I realized that you cannot tell when one ends and the other begins. Why? Because both are meshed together or intertwined.

The apostle Paul makes the statement, "...to the intent that now the manifold wisdom of God might be made known by the Church to the principalities and powers in the heavenly places..." (Eph. 3:10). Consider the "many folded" wisdom of God. I want you to imagine a standard sheet of paper. Fold it once, fold it again, fold it a third time. Keep folding until you can't fold it anymore. Now as you unfold it, each fold reveals a different section of the same piece of paper. When folded, only one section of the paper is visible, yet each unfolding reveals a new area. So it is with the wisdom of God. Everything is not on the surface. There are some things that remain a paradox (a truth that appears to be self-contradictory on the outside, yet if we keep unfolding, we find it doesn't contradict at all).

Specific wisdom or truth that is revealed to us is probably the culmination of many other truths tied together, truths that are unseen or not understood at the moment.

For instance, it is a truth that God gives us the ability to get wealth (see Deut. 8:18), yet people are poor. I've heard this biblical truth quoted many times. I've even quoted it myself. It's a good Scripture to teach and quote, especially during the offering time. Why? Because it's true. God does give us the ability to get wealth. The paradox is that there are people who are homeless, people who still live in poor sections of town, people who still are on welfare and fixed incomes. Do they have the ability to get wealth! Of course! But they're poor. Now we can justify their situation by explaining that they just are not applying God's principles. But the fact remains, you have two truths: God gives the ability to get wealth, yet there are poor people. Of course, wealth demands proper financial management, among other things. This is a truth, but it is an unseen truth. It is a truth that may be deep within the folds.

Now that I think about it, this was probably the missing equation in my conversation with John. John didn't have all of the answers, and I certainly didn't either. But who said it's a sin not to have all the answers? Jesus once said to His disciples that He had more things to tell them, more things to explain, but at the moment they were unable to grasp them.

I'll never forget a gentleman who became a member of our church. One day he approached me and said, "You know, Pastor, I like the preaching, the teaching, the music and the people. The only thing I'm having a problem with is that you ask for money every single service. Why do you always have to ask for so much money?" I tried to explain to him that we don't just ask for money every service, that offerings are a part of what worship is all about. We don't give money merely to keep the electricity flowing or the water running, although these things are necessities. We give because the Word commands it. Now he heard what I said, but he couldn't grasp it.

When we come to understand that we understand very little, then we have reached the plane where God can act. The apostle Paul had a unique way of putting it: "For we know in part and we prophesy in part" (I Cor. 13:9). He goes on to say, "When I was a child, I spoke as a child, I understood as a child, I thought as a child; but when I became a man, I put away childish things" (vs. 11). Notice the phrase, "when I was..."; the word *was* is the past tense. In the phrase, "but when I became..." the word *became* indicates a process of development.

In the American way of thinking, everything should be instant. When I put food in the microwave for two minutes, I sometimes get frustrated because it takes too long! We have commercials that advertise stores geared for "people who can't wait." When we buy groceries, it's not enough to go to a market anymore; we must go to a supermarket, and in each supermarket there is an express line for purchases of ten items or fewer and a line where you pay only cash. This speeds up the checkout.

Unfortunately, we carry this same instant mentality into Christianity. We see the Christian faith as something to attain and the teaching of the Word of God as something to acquire, within two years or less. If things don't happen very quickly for us, then we feel either that we've lost our joy or that it's time to move from one church to another.

When we learn that God cannot be contained in our doctrinal and theological "boxes," then we will realize that Christianity is not something we acquire, but something we experience. Faith in Jesus Christ is not what we put into our pockets, but what we do. Life in God is how we live and how we move from faith to faith, from glory to glory.

There is never an end to God. If we ever were to come to an end in God, then God would cease to be God. We are constantly "unfolding that sheet of paper." We are constantly seeing the magnitude of the beauty of God. You can stare at a diamond for hours and see colors each minute that you did not see before. So it is with the Christian life, we are developing every day. We are learning and unlearning what we have learned before, in order to learn again.

During each of our worship services we have a section that we call the Prayer of Faith. This is when we pray for people who are sick or hurt, going through financial strain or divorce or experiencing various circumstances. Now this is common and normal to us, but people who visit our church having different spiritual and liturgical backgrounds find it a little confusing. People who come to Abundant Life Cathedral from churches different from ours may even find it shocking and offensive to pray directly for the sick (that is, unless they are the one who's very sick).

At first, I could not understand this attitude. I could not understand why anyone would feel intimidated by our praying for the sick. After all, the Bible says we are supposed to do it. Later I realized that, as a church, we had traveled a long road of Scripture and revelation. We had layered our beliefs to this point. If these people had grown up in our church and had had our experiences, then they would have understood our position. It's like the difference between newlyweds and a couple experiencing their 25th anniversary. You will never be able to explain to newlyweds that after 25 years marriage takes on a different character.

When Saundra and I were first married, my mother-in-law told me that as you get older, intimacy gets better. Now we were young, and we felt we had it all together. We just knew, we knew that we knew! After all, we were young and in love, and they were old fogeys and not really tuned in to what was happening. As we approached our 15th anniversary I realized that the relationship between my wife and me had grown deeper; therefore, intimate experiences, which are merely the manifestation of what takes place inwardly, naturally were getting better as the relationship grew.

This is development. This is unfolding the ways of God. This is taking the time to study each petal on a rose. This is taking the time to notice each sunset. This is taking the time to realize that creation is a conglomeration of intricate beauties that never will be exhausted.

So what do I tell the "Johns" of this generation? What do I tell people who have tried over and over again to fit the pieces of life's puzzle together? I tell them that God is the "ultimate equalizer," and nothing escapes His view. Nothing gets past Him, and what may seem to be an unresolved situation will find its resolution in God.

The answer is not always in praying for the obvious; the answer many times is in praying for illumination. The apostle Paul prayed that the eyes of the people in the church at Ephesus would be opened and that their minds would be illuminated.

This is where we will find the miracles. Miracles will explode upon us when God begins to open our eyes to the deeper truths, rather than allow us to be satisfied with surface answers. It's when God begins to unfold the "sheet of paper"—His Word—and aids us in understanding that, as we continue to unfold His truths, we will find the answers to the most perplexing questions of life.

Learn to relax in Christ. In an "instant" generation, in which we think we don't have the time to wait, I submit that you do have time. When we come into a relationship with Jesus Christ, we are birthed into the sphere of eternity.

Every year on my birthday people tease me and say, "Do you know that one day you are going to reach the 'big four-o'?" I smile because I look forward to it. I do not see myself as a creature declining because of the years that are adding up; I see myself getting younger. We are not merely creatures of time, but also creatures of eternity. We have forever to fulfill our God-given destinies. We have time!

Take God out of the box. I have decided to let God be who He is. After all, He's going to do it anyway. One of the most precious things that can be done is to unfold the wisdom and beauty of God each day in a manner that was not done the day before.

Recognize that you have time. The apostle Paul once said, "For to me, to live is Christ, and to die is gain" (Phil. 1:21). Death is merely an interruption in the process of living. On the other side of every death is a resurrection. Therefore, time is not a problem for us. We have plenty of it. Yes, it hurts when we don't find the answers immediately, but relax, God is larger than your box.

Dear God, open my eyes, let me see Your beauties from day to day. Let me catch a fresh glimpse of Your marvelous mercies every morning as I awaken. Open my eyes that I might see what I have never seen before. I trade in my time for Your priceless gift of eternity. Teach me to relax in You, for I trust that every day with You will be sweeter than the day before. Amen.

7

God Still Thinks He's God

In addition to all finite selves there is a being called God, numerically distinct from them, an independent centre of consciousness, with his own unique life and purposes, with a differential activity of his own.

Charles A. Bennett

It must be tough being God. The work load is enough to make mere mortals scream, let alone the hours! Can you imagine listening to millions of people at the same time, 24 hours a day, and having to turn down the majority of the requests because the people could really handle the problem themselves? God has to do this forever, and He knows that He has to do so. Perish the thought!

How does it feel to be God and know You're God? Who knows how He got the job? He just...did! Nobody can tell Him what to do.

Imagine God being examined by a psychiatrist. Let's call the psychiatrist "Dr. Sure."

Dr. Sure opens the dialogue saying, "Welcome, uh...what do You prefer to be called?"

"I have many names—Jehovah, Elohim, El Shaddai— and some you couldn't pronounce even if you tried, but just plain God will be fine."

The psychiatrist considers Him a basket case, but he thinks, *Why not continue the interview? Who knows? It might be fun, and a quick buck could be made at the same time.*

"Well, uh...God, is it?"

"Yes!"

"What do all of these names mean?"

Obviously, Dr. Sure thinks, *I could end this conversation right here by diagnosing the case as one of multiple personalities.*

God replies, "In answer to your question, My names mean that I am the ultimate source of power, the ultimate source of peace, providence, love, righteousness, healing, etc., etc., etc.—you know the story."

The psychiatrist persists.

"How did all of this get started?"

"Do you know what you're asking?"

Dr. Sure apparently is disturbed by the question. *After all,* he thinks, *this is my profession. I know what I'm doing.*

"I assure You, Sir, I know my job."

God shrugs. "There never has existed a time when I didn't exist. You exist in a world of calendars, clocks and appointment books. I, well, I just exist. There never has been a moment when I have not been conscious of Myself. Darkness and chaos can surround Me, but I live in light; I am the single flame in infinite nothingness. I dwell in the flicker of a star and the entire spectrum of a rainbow. I am always pregnant, because I'm the Father and Mother of all you perceive. My worlds are unending; they span the universe as grains of sand on a seashore. I am protective of My words, for when released, they become the effervescent cause of all you see around you. I am the nucleus of the atom, the force that propels energy. Yet, I maintain My own identity apart from what I do. Shall I go on?"

Dr. Sure drops his pen. He was nervously manipulating it between his thumb and index finger when it slipped. He conspicuously retrieves it.

"Well, hum...hum...," he clears his throat. "I think I understand Your, uh...perspective. So tell me, how long have You been this way?"

"I told you: forever, if you can conceive of 'foreverness.'"

"Tell me, God, what else can You do?"

"I can do whatever I want to do."

"Does everyone approve of the things You do?"

"No, I get resistance every now and then."

"Why is that?"

"Well, the things I do or allow to be done have a tendency to disturb a lot of people."

Dr. Sure smiles with relief. He knows he's regaining his composure.

"I've got You there."

"How's that?"

"Isn't God supposed to do things that benefit His creation?"

"Of course," God says, "I've never failed in that department."

"Well, I beg to differ. Remember what You told Your people when they were about to make war on a small city called Jericho?"

God reflects for a moment...Jericho was the sight of one of the bloodiest battles in Israel's history. God had assured Joshua that He had given His people the city. Israel's army marched around the wall seven times, and through a miraculous series of events, the walls of the city fell down flat. Ultimately, thousands in the city were killed when Joshua's army took over. God knew what Dr. Sure was getting at, so He asked,

"What's your point?"

"It doesn't seem very beneficial to help people kill other people, does it?"

"On the contrary," God replied, "it was quite beneficial."

"How can You say that?"

"Because I'm God!"

"Sir, I respect the fact that You believe You are who You say You are. But does being God give You the right to do what You want to do?"

"Of course." After a stony silence, Dr. Sure continued.

"But why?

"Because I know what makes the universe function."

"Even if what You do is wrong?" Dr. Sure countered.

"I define right and wrong."

"So You live by Your own rules of right and wrong?"

"Of course, I do. The balance of all life depends upon it."

"Tell me, God, is killing wrong?"

"Of course, it is. Thou shalt not kill."

Dr. Sure was about to find a hole in God's flawless logic.

"So You're admitting You were wrong in sending Joshua and his men to take over Jericho?"

"No, of course not. I knew what I was doing."

"God, I'm trying to comprehend this, but I don't understand Your reasoning."

"I know, but that's why I'm God. I have this uncanny ability to see future results as present realities."

The afternoon is spent, and God's hour is almost up. Dr. Sure has another patient, and it is time to wrap up this session.

"Uh...well, God," Dr. Sure removes his eyeglasses from his lips after nibbling on the tip of the left earpiece, "Your hour is up. Come see me next week at this same time, and we'll continue the discussion. I've got to prepare for my next patient, so would You mind showing Yourself to the door, disappearing, vanishing or whatever it is You do, while I update Your file?"

God doesn't vanish, but chooses to walk out the office door. After all, cheap tricks aren't His style.

Dr. Sure writes in his file, "Acute symptoms of a Supreme Being complex—He thinks He's God."

This is a very silly illustration. Of course, we would never find God on the couch of a psychiatrist, and it would be highly improbable that we would get this far in questioning God, but it brings me to a very important point. *God is who He says He is.* One of the hardest things for the human mind to accept is that God is who He says He is. Regardless of our concepts or ideas about Him, He is still God, and that means He does what He wants to do, when He wants to do it and how He wants to do it.

The "God things" that God does or at least allows to be done always shatter our concepts of how He operates.

I remember a fellow I'll call "Zeek." Although Zeek is not his real name, Zeek is a real person. Zeek had a problem—he had AIDS. At the release of this book, I don't know whether Zeek is dead or alive; whatever the case, I will speak of Zeek as living.

On several occasions, Zeek attended our church. I remember his frail frame. I recall the splotches on his face and hands. I remember that look in his eyes, as though there were someone on the inside wanting to live, but the body refused to allow it. His gaze was hollow, but in spite of it all, Zeek was a very likeable fellow. Actually, he was a person of rare spirit and courage.

I don't recall ever meeting any of Zeek's family, although occasionally he introduced me to a friend. Basically Zeek had no family other than his church.

Over the years, I have prayed for Zeek and many like him. Some have lived, but most have died. I must admit, every time I prayed for Zeek I wondered if I would ever see him again. On top of his medical problems, Zeek had a slight mental disorder; I'm not sure whether it was a result of the disease or a condition from birth.

At times, Zeek would call from the hospital, crying out in sheer pain. I could feel the pain as though I were there. Tears would well in my eyes, because each time I expected never to hear from Zeek again. But I always did! Zeek just would not die!

Zeek was not considered to be an outstanding Christian by some standards. He did not attend church often, nor did he always have a Bible in his hand. Zeek did not have a fountain of Bible verses constantly spewing from his memory. He was not the picture that most people would paint of a Christian.

I often wondered why Zeek continued to live, while others who were seemingly stronger Christians passed away? I found some sort of understanding in a passage that said, "The secret things belong to the Lord our God, but those things which are revealed belong to us..." (Deut. 29:29).

God knows about your situation. Oral Roberts once told me, "There are situations that only God knows about, and we must rest in the fact that God knows something about this that we don't." To some, this may be a very simplistic answer. But there comes a time in all of our lives that, regardless of how much we have studied or how profound we are in our thinking, we have to admit that many of the questions in life just are not answerable.

Of course, God does not want us to stop seeking. I believe God wants us to ask questions. I believe God wants us to look into the things that other men have called blasphemous. God created us to have dominion, to subdue the earth and to extend His thoughts and ways beyond our tiny circles. God created us to think; He wants us to think. He wants us to use our mind, our knowledge, our science, our intuition and our personalities to explore the unknown. By searching, we oftentimes stumble upon the answers that were there all the time. I don't believe that it's blasphemy to question the things of God. For He has said, in so many words, ask and I'll tell you; seek, you'll figure it out; knock and a world of doors will be opened to you (my paraphrase of Matt. 7:7; Luke 11:9).

God is presently at work behind the scenes. God is sovereign. In our age of technology and human enlightenment, we tend to forget that God is far beyond our human thinking.

While speaking as the mouthpiece of God, an ancient prophet once said, "...so are My ways higher than your ways, and My thoughts than your thoughts" (Isa. 55:9). As the distance between the heavens and the earth, so are my concepts in distance from yours. This passage of Scripture tells me that God thinks and acts on high levels.

There's a little illustration I use about a young man who stopped at a very busy intersection during rush hour when a traffic light stalled. He waited for about three minutes, but the light didn't change. The horns were blowing, and the people behind him were shaking their fists. Finally, he decided to go through the light. When he turned the corner, he noticed an accident, a five-car pileup. From the look of the accident, it was serious, maybe involving the loss of lives. He noticed a helicopter flying high above and quickly searched the radio stations for a traffic report. He later heard, "There's been a terrible accident at the corner of Fifth and Main. Please avoid the area, if you can. Traffic is backed up for a mile...." Thank God he hadn't disregarded the traffic signal. Had he gone ahead 30 seconds earlier, he would have been a victim of that five-car pileup and possibly could have lost his life.

We can use this as an illustration of how God sees. God saw the stalled traffic light, He saw the people cursing the stalled traffic light, and He saw a car running through an intersection and causing a fatal traffic accident. He also was aware of how a life was saved because of what seemed to be an inconvenient circumstance.

Just as the helicopter was high above the traffic situation, so God's ways are above man's. In so many words,

God is in the helicopter! There may be things around the corner in life that only God can see. So don't be frustrated, trust the "Pilot in the helicopter." Trust the voice of God. Seemingly adverse circumstances or situations are not always to your detriment; they could be for your good. God is sovereign, and He knows the outcome. The word *sovereign* means "one that exercises supreme authority and undisputed ascendancy."

We must again learn to fear God, not in terms of fright, but in terms of respect. I often use the example that when you turn on an electric fan, it will give you a cool breeze. If you use the fan properly, it will make you comfortable, but if you stick your finger into it, the blades will, without mercy, cut it off. As long as you have respect for the fan, it will benefit you, but the moment you abuse it or take it for granted, it will hurt you. I am not saying that God is out to get us, but what we must understand is that God is bigger than we are. God has the potential to squash us like ants! Now I don't fear that He will squash me, but I kind of like to keep that in mind, you understand!

Does God cause or allow disasters? To say that God *causes* disasters is to put the blame on Him. To say God *allows* disasters tells us that God either is in agreement with the outcome or cannot do anything to stop it. So either way, we have questions.

Why did Jesus one day pass by many sick people at a pool only to heal one man? The simplest answer is because He's God! It seems to me that God should heal all, help all, provide for all and talk to all. After all, He needs as many believers as He can get!

How many people have given up on God because He failed to prevent a child from being killed by a car or because He allowed the fatal heart attack of a father who was the bread winner of a family? How many people have questioned God's love because of the failure of a business that was a person's only means of support, or because of the eviction of a young family who wound up homeless because they had nowhere else to go? These are unanswerable things, secret things, and they belong to God.

I think one of the greatest illustrations that we can find is in the Scriptures concerning Jesus and a very close friend by the name of Lazarus. Jesus was in a town called Bethany, when the news came to him that Lazarus was very sick. Lazarus' two sisters, Mary and Martha, had sent the news of his sickness in such a way as to tell Jesus, "Listen, You're a close friend of ours, You heal sick people, so You'd better come now because we don't know how long he is going to last." But Jesus said something very strange, "This sickness is not unto death, but for the glory of God, that the Son of God may be glorified through it" (John 11:4).

Now according to this passage of Scripture, Jesus said, "This sickness is not unto death....," but later on Jesus said that Lazarus had fallen asleep. The disciples did not understand Jesus' terminology, so finally Jesus broke it down and told them, "Lazarus is dead." In yet another passage in the same chapter, it says that Lazarus died. Still another Scripture tells us that Mary and Martha told Jesus that had He been there, their brother would not have died (verse 21). After Jesus arrived, He asked where they had laid him or where the tomb was. The response was, "Lord by this time there is a stench, for he has been dead four days" (John 11:39b). So it is a fact that Lazarus was dead. But earlier Jesus had said that the sickness was not unto death. Now according to our thoughts and our ways, if Jesus had said the sickness was not unto death, but Lazarus died, then on the surface, it would appear that the Word (Jesus is the Living Word) did not work.

Verse 4 of John chapter 11 says, "This sickness is not unto death...." In The Amplified Bible it reads, "This sickness is not to end [or to fulfill its purpose] in death...." The higher thought is that this whole incident is not going to end in death; even though Lazarus would go through death, it would not end that way. So why didn't Jesus heal him? Well, the answer is simple: the *purpose* of God was not to heal Lazarus, but to raise him from the dead. Jesus could have sent His word and healed him. On another occasion, He had just spoken the word and a soldier's servant was healed some distance away. But had Jesus done that in Lazarus' case, He would have gone against the will of the Father, and Jesus would never do that.

Now this does not mean that Jesus wasn't sympathetic to Mary and Martha's need. After all, Mary, Martha and Lazarus were His very close friends. Jesus often stayed at their home, and they would fix meals for Him and His disciples. But sympathy and friendship were not the issue. Evidently, tapping into the purpose of God was so awesome that Jesus even allowed His close friends to go through the traumatic experience of a funeral.

Of course, we rejoice that Lazarus was raised from the dead, this was a miracle. Yet, there are still two facts that remain. First, Jesus was a healer, and Mary, Martha and His disciples knew He was. Yet, Jesus did not heal Lazarus the way they had seen Him heal others. Second, not only did Lazarus die, but he died sick. This tells us that the Word was not sent to heal him. Why? Because the Word was sent to resurrect him.

God's Word does not lack power, but God determines the use of His Word according to His own reasons. God's ways are higher than our ways, and His thoughts are higher than our thoughts. God sees "from the helicopter," while we can only see what is in front of us. God sees around the corners what we are yet to approach.

As in the situation between Jesus and Lazarus, we wonder why a child is killed by a car. In such tragic moments, we do not understand and wonder why God did not prevent it. It is at moments like this that we ask the question, "Where can I find a place to stand?" The answer is that we must learn to rest in the fact that God is God.

The Final Session

It's been a week now, and it's time for God's final session with Dr. Sure. God walks in, takes the couch, and the questions begin again. Dr. Sure picks up where he left off:

"Last time, we spoke about creation, killing, right and wrong. Tell me, what is Your greatest fear?"

"I have none."

"Oh, come on, there must be one?"

"Of course, I'm aware fear exists. It's all over My creation, but personally, I have none."

"Then what about the fear of people not believing in You?"

God remains expressionless. The sheer power of His confidence fills the room so that Dr. Sure can feel it. God responds with the assurance of someone who has a carefully laid plan.

"All will believe in Me at some point. Some now, some later, but ultimately all will believe."

Dr. Sure clicks on a video with his remote control. On the TV screen is a well-groomed evangelist praying for the sick. A commentator interviews six of these people concerning the results of the evangelist's prayers. It seems they were not healed, and some of the family members even report cases of their relatives dying after the prayers.

God does not blink an eye. Dr. Sure turns the video off and says,

"What about all of Your believers dying after so many people have prayed for them to live?"

"My believers never die; they live on. Death is nothing to fear. I have taken care of it."

Dr. Sure is now grabbing at straws.

"Then what about Your churches closing down. I've heard that..."

"Church buildings closing down don't bother Me. I don't live in buildings anyway."

Dr. Sure wants to go for the jugular vein.

"You've heard, as well as I have, that You have been having trouble with some of Your preachers lately. What are You going to do about it?"

"No need to worry. I know how to take care of My own."

"No need to worry? What about evil and corruption taking over?"

"That will never happen."

"And how can You be so sure?"

"Because I have fixed it."

Dr. Sure drops his tone of voice and poises himself for the last question.

"Well, it's been a pleasure talking with You, but our time is just about up. Now this does not mean I believe You're God, but, off the record, You do seem very assured of Yourself. If You are in so much control, why is Your world so out of control?"

God waits. This is the only time during the interview that He waits. He turns His head toward Dr. Sure and, in a very deep, passionate tone, says, "My son, it's all a matter of perspective. Before joy, there is weeping; before victory, there is always war; before the birth of something new, there must always be the pain of labor. Even that which seems out of control resides yet in the sphere of My control. You see, I have seen the end from the beginning, and since the beginning, I have always known I win."

"And what makes You so sure of that?"

"I'm God, and that is all the assurance necessary."

8

When Brooks Dry Up

Isn't it fascinating how we portray many biblical characters as sane and perfect people? Now I don't mean to degrade biblical characters, but we often translate them into the world of the superhuman. If we actually take the time to look deep into their lives, we will see that they are ordinary human beings struggling with some of life's most perplexing questions. One of the questions that comes to mind is: What do we do when our sources of *income*, *health* and *support* actually dry up? I believe one of the best persons to answer this is a man by the name of Elijah.

Now, of course, we know Elijah is a very popular biblical character, and his name is recognized immediately. As the account in First Kings chapter seventeen relates, centuries ago, there was a man named Ahab who had some weather problems. Well, let me go back a little and explain.

Ahab was a king, but he was a king who was not very popular with the Jewish people of his time. Ahab married a woman by the name of Jezebel. (How often do we hear the name Jezebel? Not much. Very few people name their daughters Jezebel, because of the stigma that goes with the name.) Jezebel believed in gods made of stone and wood, in other words, idols. Because of their marriage, Ahab gradually began to practice some of the same things that Jezebel and her people practiced. Then there was Elijah. Elijah was considered to be a spokesman for Jehovah (God). So, we now have three main characters: Ahab, Jezebel and Elijah.

Elijah was told by God to tell Ahab that it was not going to rain for about three years. The reason for the drought was to break the reign of idolatry in the land. Elijah walked into the king's court and said, "It's not going to rain...." Now that was a very startling weather report, especially when rain was so important to the growing of crops and the nourishment of their country. But it was more important that idolatry be broken, in order for God to continue to be recognized as the Source for Israel.

After Elijah had said these very startling words to Ahab, God told him not to live in the immediate vicinity. The reason probably was to avoid the chopping block! Elijah was told to relax and live next to a small brook. Every day Elijah would get up in the morning, take a drink from the brook, and then ravens would feed him flesh in the morning and flesh in the evening. But one day when the prophet woke up, as he wiped sleep from his eyes, he found that the brook had dried up (verse 7).

Many think that just because things don't work out to their benefit, God has somehow walked away. So many times, people blame it on "the devil," but the devil may not have had anything to do with it. Now I realize that satan is connected to lies, contentions, conflicts, poverty, sickness and every malady within our society, but we cannot spend our lives blaming the devil for everything. If we mismanage our money, it does not mean that the devil stole it. If we do not take care of our bodies, it does not mean that the devil stole our health. Often, we have placed ourselves in these predicaments. But what causes us to raise an eyebrow is when circumstances arise that have nothing to do with the devil, little to do with us, and all to do with something God has said.

The brook was Elijah's present source of sustenance; it was his source of life. For a period of time, he had come to depend upon it. He expected its waters to be there.

Every day we expect certain things in life. A wife expects a husband to be there when she needs him; a husband expects a wife to be a shoulder to cry on when he needs her. We expect to go to our job every morning when we wake up. Children expect their parents to be available. As a nation, we expect the government to bail us out, whether it involves welfare or savings and loan institutions! Husbands, wives, family, parents, government, job, career, education and so many other things are expected to be available to us under normal circumstances. These are sources of life and can be considered to be our brooks. Yet, how often do these brooks dry up?

Even though the brook was a blessing to Elijah, God still allowed it to dry up. This reminds us that even though certain areas in our lives are a present blessing, God will allow them to dry up. Elijah was human, just as we are, and our brooks (sources of life) will dry up, just as Elijah's did.

So why did the brook dry up? Simple. There was no rain in the land! Many times we search for some in-depth answer or some unknown revelation to explain the phenomenon of brooks drying up. But the brook dried up because there was no rain. Even good, hard-working Christians can and will be affected by natural phenomena in their sphere of life.

I live in an area called the Lone Star State, Texas, and it's a well-known fact that huge amounts of oil gush from here. During the late seventies and early eighties there was something called an "oil boom." People from all over the country and even the world were moving to Texas. They were looking for *sources of life,* a "brook." They were looking for income. They were looking for the ability to settle down and have a better quality of life. But around 1982, Texas experienced something called "the oil bust." The price of oil went through the ceiling, and there were very long gasoline lines around the country. It was reported that the oil industry was having some very difficult times in obtaining oil (the purpose of this book is not to discuss whether the oil shortage was real or unreal, ha! ha!). Many oil workers were transferred to other cities, and people were laid off from jobs that centered around the oil industry.

I recall a local church in our community that had been growing at "light speed." This church was located in an area where many oil workers and oil executives lived. When the oil bust took place, the church decreased in attendance by half and likewise experienced a financial decrease. The church had recently bought a large piece of property, but because income had dropped by 50 to 75 percent, the church was unable to pay the note. Consequently, the congregation had to move to smaller facilities.

Tell me, was it the will of God for the church's income to drop? Was it the will of God for the church's attendance to drop? Was it the will of God for the church to lose much of its influence in the community? I don't think so. So why did it happen? It happened because of a natural phenomenon. The oil, or the brook, dried up!

Can we blame this on the devil? Of course we can, indirectly. Satan is responsible for whatever shortages or corruption in the oil industry there might have been. Yet, other churches attended by people of lesser means grew, while this very well-to-do church declined.

This is not hard to understand. Sources dry up all the time. Everyone encounters this at one time or another. Layoffs take place in major corporations because of low product demand. Departments cut back workers because of improper management or a lack of sound structure. Budget cuts come from home offices, government and state headquarters all the time. Insurance costs are skyrocketing as liabilities increase. The "good ol' boy" syndrome can cause people of different races and cultures to lose out economically. Marriages that started off with big beautiful weddings wind up in divorce courts because of financial strain. When there is a war, our young men and women must leave their civilian jobs in order to participate in a conflict overseas; however, when they come back home, they may find that their jobs have either been filled or just simply erased. Overseas production can cause sources to dry up because of the demand for foreign products by Americans who bypass products made in the United States.

Why does it seem that my source is cut off? Well, it may not necessarily be the devil, yourself or even God; it may be caused by natural circumstances. At times you may even find that your source dries up because of the move of God in the earth. In other words, God may be fixing something.

When we think of God, we have a tendency to think of absolute perfection. We don't expect God to die; we don't expect God to contradict Himself. We don't expect God to make mistakes, break down, react unfairly, become quick tempered or to discriminate. Of course, these character-istics have never fit God. God is perfect, and when I speak of perfection I mean complete. Consequently, we logically presume that anything a perfect God creates also must be perfect. After all, we have read in the Bible that "Every good gift and every perfect gift is from above..." (James 1:17). But the fact of the matter is that everything within the confines of creation is not necessarily perfect. There is hunger; there is proverty; there is sickness. There is dis-ease, tragedy, awkwardness, prejudice and the possibility of bank computer errors!

So what about a perfectly healthy newborn who grows up to murder his parents because he needs to feed a ruthless addiction? What about a young child who makes perfect grades, runs with the perfect crowd, nightly reads the Bible about a perfect God, yet finds out there's cancer in his body only to die before he learns to live? What about an individual who has a perfect relationship that blossoms into a perfect marriage, but finds that the perfect spouse has infected her with AIDS? So much for perfection.

God has never sought perfect people. On the contrary, God tends to use imperfect people in imperfect situations in order to work a perfect plan. God uses imperfect people to fix a planet filled with imperfect things. Why does God take the time to fix imperfect things? Because He is determined to unfold His perfect plan.

Remember the story in the Book of Numbers, chapter fourteen, concerning the children of Israel standing on the edge of the Promised Land, but unwilling to enter? God's perfect plan was for His people to go into the land. His perfect plan was for them to take the cities, live in the cities and enjoy the benefits. But because of unbelief, fears and doubts, the will of the nation was broken. They became a broken people with broken visions and broken plans. It was up to God to fix the brokenness in order to complete His plan for His people.

Tell me, have you ever come face to face with broken dreams or broken visions, while all the time standing on the edge of victory? Well, I have, and many others would stand in agreement with me.

God had a plan, and the plan was to start with a new generation of Israelites. God had decided to let the generation of doubters die in the wilderness, while the younger generation grew old enough to fight and enter the Promised Land. The death of the older generation seemed harsh, so why did God allow it to happen? Because God was fixing something all along.

Going back to our story about Elijah, we find that God's judgment was upon Ahab. The sentence was no rain in the land for three years.

When difficult times come, don't always take it personally. God's ultimate goal will always be greater than the "in-between" circumstances.

God told Elijah how to deal with the dried-up brook— He told him to leave it, in other words, to leave the dead source of provision, and go to a widow's house in a city called Zarephath (verse 9).

Can you imagine what was going on in Elijah's mind? He was probably thinking, *I can't believe this. One moment I'm drinking water from a brook, being fed by a bunch of scavenger birds, and the next moment I'm without any source of life—no food, no water, no income. If God can cause ravens to feed me, why can't He keep the brook flowing?*

In our journey with God, I believe there are those special times, those forks in the road, those nagging tugs and unrelenting pushes that challenge us to new places in Him. There are places in God we would never venture into on our own, except for a few dried-up brooks.

This particular dried up brook took Elijah to the home of a poor, helpless widow who had literally given up on life. What a great pair, a starving widow and a prophet who was down on his luck! Yet, when circumstances are at their worst, God is at His best. God functions in some of the most unlikely places. These unlikely places are the first steps in a spiritual journey that leads to God's ultimate plan for us. We may not like the steps, but each one is necessary.

Take Larry for instance. Larry is unemployed, so he prays, expecting a "higher power" to help him land that one-in-a-million job. All of a sudden, McDonald's calls! Then there's Ann, who has been waiting for God to send her the right husband. Just when she's about to give up, this ugly, I mean, u-g-l-y, man with a tie that doesn't even match his suit comes into her life, and the funny thing is, he's nice! What about Louis and Sharon, who have been searching for a house, but an apartment opens up first? Ronald has an excellent voice and probably could earn a living in the entertainment field, but he winds up singing second tenor, not first, but second tenor, in the church choir. These incidents just seem to be "adding insult to injury," but the events in each of these cases are only steps to the top.

I can hear you saying, "Aw, come on, how can this be God, especially if I feel like I'm going through hell?" Well, so did Elijah! He went to a city called Zarephath, which translates, "the crucible." Webster's Dictionary defines *crucible* as a "container made of granite, porcelain or other substance that can resist great heat for melting ores and metals." In other words, it is a place or thing in which metal is heated to its hottest point, until all of the impurities come to the surface. The impurities are skimmed off, thus leaving pure metal. Another definition is "a severe test; hard trial." The root word *cruci* is also found in the word *crucifix*, cross, or the place of testing. This is what Elijah was involved in. Elijah felt like he was in hell, while unknowingly he was coming closer to a miracle.

Life takes us to these unusual places. There is nothing strange about moments and times of testing. It's when we feel that we are in the deepest pit of hell, literally about to be destroyed, that God meets us.

Let's put this story in perspective.

1. Both the widow and Elijah were experiencing the effects of the drought.

2. Both of them had come to the end of their source of sustenance.

3. Both of them were hungry.

4. Both of them needed a miracle.

5. Both of them had to decide on a course of action.

Normally, we would follow a story like this in chronological order. If you're a trained speaker or lecturer, that's what you would do. But let's jump ahead and peek at the outcome of this dilemma in First Kings 17:16.

Blessed verse 16! The Bible tells us that the widow watched her meal barrel and oil jar miraculously refill itself after every use. Talk about "30 percent more free?" Oh, how I would love to see my checkbook replenish itself after every use! Verse 16 is the miracle. This tells us that Elijah and the widow were destined for provision. It tells us that God intervened.

I travel a lot and usually purchase my airplane tickets as early as possible in order to enjoy substantial savings. The airline or travel agency mails the tickets directly to my office, but they also enclose a very important piece of information. It's called the itinerary. Now the itinerary tells me that if I board a specific plane at a specific time, then I will deplane that same aircraft at a future time and future destination; this could be called my destiny.

Verse 16 in this story was the destination or destiny of the widow and Elijah. There is no way in the world that they could have known what would take place. It was destined that Elijah would eat, the widow would eat and that they both would survive the drought.

While standing in the airport waiting for my plane to leave, I became aware of the fact that planes were leaving for certain destinations every hour on the hour. I noticed the multiplicity of destinations to the East and West coast, London, Paris, Mexico, South America, etc. Although planes were taking off for a specific destination every hour, I still remained in Houston. The only way to get to one of those destinations was to board one of those planes. Now verse 16 was the destination, but Elijah and the widow had to get on the plane of present events, figuratively speaking, and ride out the circumstances.

This unlocks a much deeper understanding of the Bible as a book of destiny. It is a book that takes us from one place to another. It is the account of man coming from God and ultimately going back to God; that's his destination. But in between, there are a lot of circumstances that don't seem to point to the ultimate destination. Since the entire Bible is a book of destiny, in order for us to arrive at the places advertised, we must "get on the plane" or "board" His Word. So what do we do when our brooks dry up? Remember what God has said.

Some of you are asking the question, "How can I hear God speak, or if He is speaking, how can I be sure that what I think He's saying is really what He's saying?" We can go to the Bible for the answer.

Although the words of the Bible are hundreds, even thousands, of years old, they are just as effective in the present as they were in the past. Why? Because words carry spirit and thought.

Let me upset some religious thinking here. The Bible is nothing more than paper, ink and a little glue to hold it together. Now this takes nothing away from the Bible, because the Bible is what it is. It's a book, and the words are what they are—words. Words are like a conveyor belt in an assembly line. A conveyor belt carries a product from point A to point B. Words convey or carry a thought or idea from one point to another.

Take John 1:1, for instance. It says, "In the beginning was the Word, and the Word was with God, and the Word was God." This tells us that words are the containers of thoughts, ideas and intents. John 1:14 says, "...the Word became flesh and dwelt among us, and we beheld His glory...," which tells us that Jesus Christ (the Word made flesh) became the "conveyor belt" or the container of the expression of God to mortal man. John 6:63b relates, "The words that I speak to you are spirit, and they are life."

When we read the words of the Bible, we are not just reading a good book. When those of us who are hungry for the ideas and mind of God read the the Bible, we are allowing the spirit, intent and ideas of God to be conveyed to us.

It's interesting how one can listen to biblical teaching or preaching and, although the speaker may be talking about a number of subjects, that individual will always hear certain sentences or phrases that "come alive" only to him or her. Now everybody hears the same words, but all will grasp different ideas.

Once you hear, whatever you do, do something. Always remember that action is better than reaction. All of our lives we are taught to react to situations. Phrases from my youth that stay foremost in my mind are "Keep your eyes open," "Watch out for the muggers," "Stay on guard," "Don't fight, unless someone else starts it." Now this well may be good advice, but it merely gears our actions to the actions of others.

God did not intend for us to react; we were destined to be people of action and dominion. God has given us our own itinerary and destiny demands that we follow it.

There is a passage in the Bible that says, "The steps of a good man are ordered by the Lord..." (Ps. 37:23). To be ordered means to be directed, led or guided. God directs us by altering our course. This means that we must begin walking, regardless of the circumstances or the direction, and trust God to make the adjustments.

In August of 1972 I preached my first sermon, but at that point you would never have made me believe that I would be writing this chapter of my fifth book. Now I believe there was a direction in which God wanted me to go, but at that time, I never would have believed it would take me to this particular point in life.

There was a time the apostle Paul hated Christians! As a matter of fact, he set out on a mission to destroy as many as he could. Wouldn't you know it? God met him in the midst of a potentially tragic mission. Yet, God did not change his direction, He merely changed his mind.

How many times do we sit back and wait for things to "fall from the sky," for some answer to come out of the twilight zone, or for some miracle to billow out of a cloud? I believe it's human nature to sit down, put our chins in our hands and expect the worst. I believe it's human nature to just sit and wait for something good to come along. All of the teaching in life directs us to hope for the best, yet we expect calamity. We can't just sit around and wait. Why? Because we are creatures of God, and God is a God of constant motion.

Two years after Saundra and I started our church, it seemed as though we never would grow beyond 50 people. We would gain 10 members and lose 20! I would read books and magazine articles and talk to "successful" pastors about church growth. I couldn't wait to get back and institute those ideas in our ministry. But wouldn't you know it? They didn't seem to work. We would always wind up right back where we had started.

After two years I began to wonder, *Is God moving on our behalf?* I mean, it seemed as if God was sitting somewhere far away in a big white chair doing absolutely nothing! For months, the question kept invading my thoughts, *Why doesn't God move?*

It was during that time period (well, maybe later, I'm not sure) that I learned a powerful truth about God: God is never idle. God is always in constant motion.

Genesis 1:1-2 says, "In the beginning God created the heavens and the earth. The earth was without form, and void; and darkness was on the face of the deep. And the Spirit of God was hovering over the face of the waters." Notice that the earth was without form and void and darkness was upon the face of the deep. Now this had to be a very discouraging sight. The Hebrew word for void translates, "empty, chaotic and wasted." Not only was God aware of the chaos, but darkness covered the earth as well. This must have been a downright tragic scene!

How many times have we found ourselves in empty, chaotic, wasted and hopeless situations? Well, if you're like me—many times! On top of that, it seems as though there's no direction or purpose to any of it.

When I look at our generation, I see so much chaos. Every news report talks about impending war, political cover-ups, religious scandals or endless philosophical debates. You see lives being wasted by drugs, disease, murder and crime. When we ask for solutions, all we get are empty words. It appears as if some strange cloud of darkness covers this entire earth.

Well, in a sense that's what God saw. As human beings, we feel like throwing up our hands, shrugging our shoulders and walking away, but God didn't. The Bible says that the Spirit of God *moved* upon the face of the deep. How dramatic! Even in the midst of chaos, God was moving.

If God is a God of motion, and we are created in His image, then we, too, must be a people of motion. We must be a people of action, regardless of what circumstances dictate. We must not merely react, we should force circumstances to react to us. We are a people of innovation, because God is a God of innovation.

Chapters 1 and 2 of Genesis give us a clear picture of God's creative acts and creative power. You must remember that everything God created had not been created before. No one knew what a bird or fish looked like. They were something fresh out of the mind of God.

As human beings, we have a tendency to become stale and unimaginative. We settle for less and remain within the borders of self-imposed limitations. But God is calling His people out of those limitations. He is saying, "Get up! Stretch out! Release those eagles' wings!" Why? Because inside every believer is the ability to go beyond restrictions.

Some of you have limited yourselves to working mediocre jobs and developing mediocre families. Because of it, you have a mediocre existence. I believe the time has come to break out of the mold and cut the reins that are holding all of us back.

I grew up in a semitraditional black Baptist church. I say semitraditional because black Baptist churches differ in certain parts of the country. I was raised in one that had good singing, a loud, spirited organ, fiery preaching, a lot of hand clapping and heavy foot stomping. When I finally visited a quiet Baptist church, I really wasn't sure what I was!

As I grew older, I sensed the call of God to the ministry. It was assumed by my family, friends and even myself that I would one day become pastor of a Baptist church, and I did. But there were always the seeds of unlimited possibilities planted deep inside me. As I studied the Bible, I began to realize that there were no such things as denominations. Jesus was not coming back for a Baptist church, a Methodist church, a Pentecostal church or even a Christian center! Jesus was coming back for the Church. But what was the Church? I knew it had to be more than a building.

The twelfth chapter of the Book of First Corinthians, tells us that the Church is the Body of Christ on earth. The Church is not a physical building, but people, covenant people, who declare Jesus Christ as Lord. A denominational title doesn't make a church, "the Church." Even the word *church* comes from the Greek *ekklesia*, meaning "called out." Wherever a people who have experienced a relationship with Christ come together for a common purpose, you will find the Church.

This was to be the foundation for the organization of our church. Now I am not starting a campaign that is anti-denominational—on the contrary! At that time, I just believed God wanted to build something fresh and alive. The message of the gospel would be the same, but I believed God wanted to express it in a unique and vibrant way, through a unique and vibrant vehicle. So Abundant Life Cathedral was born.

Throughout history, God has always revealed Himself in unique and unexpected ways. Because we are His children, I believe God expects us to act in unique, innovative and unexpected ways. We can talk about it all day, but it will never happen until we do something—until we act!

God is a master strategist. It doesn't take much brain power to grasp that truth. All you've got to do is look at His well-laid plans from Genesis to the Revelation.

It's interesting how everything we do in the natural mirrors something in the spiritual. Take walking, for instance. To get from one destination to another you have to proceed step by step. One of God's interesting characteristics is that He always plans the end before He starts. Not only does He plan the end, but He also clears a series of paths that, if taken will lead us to that desired end. Each step is like a link in a chain. Every connection that is made strengthens the chain and takes us closer to the purpose for which the completed chain is designed. Success is making each connection, link by link.

I must confess that while writing this section I am watching the final quarter of a very important Houston Oilers football game. If Houston wins, they will be one step closer to the Super Bowl. Houston is now down by six points, and they need a touchdown. In order to get that touchdown, they must complete a series of plays down the football field, running and catching passes a few yards at a time. If they execute each play correctly, a touchdown is inevitable. They call this process a drive.

Successful faith is not only trusting God for an unknown end, but trusting God that we will make each connection, step by step, link by link. In other words, completing a drive.

I knew our church was destined to grow. I knew deep down inside that we would acquire property and build buildings, but I didn't know how we would do it. We now own property valued at over five million dollars. How did we do it? *Step by step.* We signed month-to-month rental agreements before we signed leases. We signed short-term leases before we signed long-term leases. We signed long-term leases before we signed bank notes. We acquired land piece by piece, acre by acre. Our goal has always been to make the proper, God-ordained connections. If the connections were made, the outcome would be the will of God.

I encourage you to not be afraid of circumstances that don't appear to be the answer to your prayers. They probably are not, but those very circumstances may lead to the answer you've prayed about.

Over the years, I've watched pastors whose goals were to build five- and ten-thousand seat church auditoriums. At one time, I was caught up in this "church boom" mania. Now there's nothing wrong with churches having thousands of members. We do, and I applaud them. But I also began to notice pastors whose memberships never reached, let's say, the two-hundred mark. They became stressed out and felt as if they had failed. Then it dawned on me, "There is no failure in a two-hundred-member congregation," but there is failure in not realizing that a two-hundred-member congregation is merely a link in a five-thousand-member chain!

I learned one principle that changed my outlook on ministry forever. Build the people and the people will build the church! The link is not numbers, the link is people. I believe the apostle Paul put all of this in its proper perspective by writing "For we know that the whole creation groans and labors with birth pangs together until now" (Rom. 8:22).

We are God's ambassadors and He teaches us to walk step by step. He does not overwhelm us with the total picture but gently nudges us on toward the next adventure, the next link in a series of planned events.

So concentrate on looking for the next link, because that link along with others, is connecting you to a magnanimous future.

And by the way, the Houston Oilers never did connect with their receivers on any of the passes. They never made a first down. They never completed the drive. They never connected the links, and consequently, never made a touchdown. Houston lost the game.

9

Releasing the Hope

...Christ in you, the hope of glory.

Colossians 1:27

This chapter is designed to cause you to dream again, to expect what, up until now, you have neglected to expect.

You have probably heard the familiar quote, "...faith is the substance of things hoped for..." (Heb. 11:1). This tells us of what "things hoped for" are made. The definition of the word *substance* is "reality...or the essential matter of a thing." Faith is the essential matter of which things are made, and not just things, but things hoped for. There is a difference.

For example, automobiles are made of metal. (Although nowadays we find them to be more plastic, let's assume for our purpose that automobiles are mostly metal.) If we were to apply our statement about faith to an automobile, it would read, "faith is the substance of automobiles." Of course, that is not true; metal is the substance of automobiles. But suppose we are living in the age of horse and buggy, long before anyone has ever dreamed of or envisioned an automobile. Metal would not be used for automobiles, because automobiles wouldn't exist. All you would have is metal, a substance. The point that I'm making is that without a dream or vision of the automobile, the metal would only be a purposeless mass or something waiting to be shaped. So it is with faith. Faith is only a "mass" without purpose, a reality without shape, that is until a dream or a vision comes along. The dream or vision is called hope. Hope is something dreamed (envisioned) or something expected.

It is our dreams and expectations that give shape, purpose and meaning to the substance called faith. Steel, iron and aluminum can be all around us, but they will never transport us anywhere, meet our need for travel, or accomplish a specific purpose, until they become an automobile. So it is with the substance called faith. Faith cannot fulfill a purpose until there is a dream, a vision or an expectation.

Faith is like cookie dough, while hope is the cookie cutter. When the cookie cutter comes into contact with the dough and creates the shape of a cookie, we can then say dough is the substance of the cookie. Without the cookie cutter providing a shape, the shapeless dough is merely a substance.

How many times have we said that God made the world out of nothing? Well, we know that to be untrue, because the Bible tells us that the world or worlds were framed by the Word of God. Planet Earth was not made from nothing, it was made from something. Faith is not some fog or mist suspended in midair, it is a substance. We may not be able to see it, but it is no less a substance. We speak of the reality of gravity, yet we can't touch it. We feel the effects of wind, yet we can't see it. Faith is the same way, it is a substance that is tangible on some other plane or dimension beyond our own.

At one time, becoming the mayor of a major city was literally out of the question for anyone of African-American descent. This was not because black Americans did not have the ability, but because of the racial climate in America. On one occasion, I remember the excitement when a black man finally became mayor. You talk about a cause for shouting in black America? Brother, it was happening! All over the city, in every pulpit, in every meeting, in every newspaper, people were talking about the first black mayor of an American city. But what we did not know was that after the first black became mayor, there would soon be a great number of others all across America. When it happened for one, then others followed suit, and not only mayors, but the first black became a quarterback in the NFL.

For years it had been echoed that the reason there were no black quarterbacks was the NFL believed blacks could not think fast enough on their feet. Now of course, we know that to be untrue, but black America sensed how the NFL felt behind closed doors. Of course, black people were enraged about it, but nobody felt that there was anything that could be done.

I look back at my father, who was an all-American athlete. He was a basketball, gymnastics and football star. He was an excellent running back, an excellent retriever, but his gift and talent was quarterbacking. However, because there were no black quarterbacks in college football (other than in black colleges) or in the NFL, he was encouraged to become a running back. Ultimately, my father left school and chose another profession. Many times I've wondered what it would have been like to have a father who was a famous quarterback. But being a quarterback was outside his hopes, dreams and expectations.

To say that the reason there were no black mayors in America was black people had no faith is untrue. Blacks needed faith just to survive the events of everyday life. They needed faith to survive economically, socially and even culturally during the peak of the civil rights activities in the sixties. Black America didn't lack faith, what it lacked in some cases was hope (dreams, visions and expectations). Black mayors, quarterbacks and governors all became a reality when there were individuals who believed they could go beyond the status quo.

When Abundant Life Cathedral was started, most people envisioned a church that was of a certain denomination. After all, these are the kinds of churches black people start, aren't they? But I had envisioned something different. I saw a church that was neither black nor white, a church that was modeled and patterned after the New Testament. I envisioned a church that was not limited to 15 or 20 people sitting in a storefront (the name used for small churches up North that were not in traditional church buildings). I saw a church that could do the things other churches could do. I envisioned carrying the gospel through television, opening schools and witnessing to multitudes of people clamoring to hear the gospel of the Kingdom.

In August of 1981, we began Abundant Life Cathedral. Now, from where did the hope for this come? It would be nice to say that I had dreamed it all by myself, but that's not true. Models were all around me, men and women who had accomplished the type of dreams that were simmering inside me. As that vision grew inside, I knew I needed substance to make it work. Faith is the substance of things hoped for (dreamed, envisioned or expected).

Saundra and I began to notice that the period of time between the appearances of blacks on Christian talk shows was rather lengthy. We couldn't understand it. We knew God was speaking to and through more than one certain race or culture, but they were never exposed through Christian media. We knew blacks were not always welcomed in the secular arenas, but why not in the Christian arenas?

Soon, all across America, blacks began to envision their own television programs which would expose black people to other black people worshiping God. Many churches that you see today on television (that are predominantly black with black pastors) are there at great cost.

While I was growing up, I remember certain spurts of excitement that took place in my household. One spurt was when I did something I was not supposed to do, and judgment came down upon me from my parents like a mighty stream! But then there was another spurt of excitement; this came whenever a black person was shown on television! Whenever somebody black was being interviewed, cast in a situation comedy or just walked past the camera on screen, you could hear my grandmother scream at the top of her voice, "Come here, come here! There's a black person on television!" Whatever anybody was doing, they dropped it and ran to the TV. I have given you this illustration to enable you to feel what it was like to be black during a particular era. No one, white or black, expected black people to be on television! Why was there so much surprise at this type of event? Because nobody expected it; few dreamed of it, and only the gifted dared hope for it at all. Yet many of these lost hope as time passed and racial views didn't change.

Hope is not lost all at once. You don't stop dreaming because of one or two setbacks; expectations are lost gradually. Just as a boat was designed to float on water, so we were designed to overcome the hopeless attitudes present in society. The only thing that can sink a boat is the water around it getting into it. The only thing that can sink our lives is the hopelessness around us getting into us. Unfortunately, we have become the victims of a slow leak.

Take a look at our social climate. In 1970, the number of men between the ages of 25 and 29 who had never been married was 20 out of 100. But in 1988, men between the ages of 25 and 29 who had never been married was a whopping 40 out of 100; it had almost doubled. Today, individuals between the ages of 18 and 29 postpone marriage because of—now note this—the "fear of divorce." Can you believe that 75 percent of males between the ages of 18 and 24 are still living at home, and 40 percent of children between the ages of 18 and 29 are children of divorced parents? Want more? Well, here's more. Individuals in this age group find dates through nightclubs, video dating services, party lines and 900 numbers (telephone dating services). To look at these statistics, we would say, "Oh, my God, what is this world coming to?

Maybe these children need us to be better role models?" But wait! When this age group was polled and asked whom they considered to be good role models, they answered "our grandparents." These statistics alone reflect the hopelessness munching away at our society. If our present cultural system has taught us anything, it has taught us to expect nothing from anyone. Therefore, we expect very little from marriage, and because of the rise in unemployment, we expect very little from our jobs.

In an earlier chapter, I talked about how an individual can be loyal to a company for 10, 20, or even 30 years, and then if that company decides to go into bankruptcy, that individual will lose all of those years of service with little more than a thank you. This type of greed and disloyalty in the work place creates an atmosphere of hopelessness among the work force. We don't expect to get the raises we once did. Every time we turn on the news, the index seems to be pointing down rather than up, consequently, we expect little from our economy.

We expect little from our neighbors. How many times have we been told the story of some young woman who has screamed rape and gone from house to house or apartment door to apartment door, crying for help, but neighbors refused to open the door or call the police for fear of being killed or attacked by the person who was attacking the victim? One day a young woman was being brutally assaulted in broad daylight on a public street, and people were walking by as if nothing were happening. When the police questioned witnesses, 80 to 90 percent of the responses were, "I just didn't want to get involved."

We expect very little from our peers in business. With all the clawing, the scratching and the biting in order to get to the top, we've seen too much. We've lost hope.

We've even lost hope that we can get fair dealings from our own government. Court cases, U. S. Senate hearings, and government cover-ups all have dismantled trust in the legal process.

But more tragic than any of this, we've come to expect very little from our churches, other than an occasional bologna sandwich to the homeless, a grocery bag at Thanksgiving or a used toy at Christmas. We don't look to our churches for very much anymore. After all, the church is only a place to go to for an hour or so to hear some inspiring words that may or may not get us through the week. Even the church is not expected to be a voice or force in our communities. We only expect it to be something that's "there" when we need it.

We expect little in terms of relationship. Men and women are fighting like cats and dogs, and it's getting worse. So much hostility is taking place between males and females, yet the main ingredient for stable homes and secure families is their strong relationships. With this kind of hostility brewing, how can the family hope to survive?

What about hope for brotherly love? Probably not today! The polarization of blacks, hispanics, whites, Asians, Jews and persons of countless other cultures is accelerating. Not only are we experiencing this in America, but also around the world. We have a tendency to think that because we go to church or have some type of spiritual awareness that we are exempt from all of this. But oh, no! Prejudice and racism are alive in the Church.

So where are we going to find "the hope?" From where is it going to be released? People say, "We've got to go back to the Church, we've got to get back to religion." But can we find it in our established churches?

Years ago I was preparing to do a revival. The pastor of the church was about 70 years old, and he had decided to give this "young man" a chance to prove himself. Well, I was expecting probably to preach for about five days, as was the norm for revivals. But the pastor quickly reminded me, "Well, son, I don't want you to do a week revival, I want you to do a two-week revival."

Now you must understand, I was a "young" evangelist, therefore, I only had about three sermons, and they were very "young!" I found out later that I was expected to preach a minimum of 16 messages. Can you imagine how I felt?

Well, to make a long story short, I did preach the messages, and I got through the revival. One of the highlights was an elderly lady who approached me one night and said, "Son, that was a good message." Now whenever an elderly woman calls you "son," get ready! I said to her,

"Well, thank you very much. I'm trying to do the best I can."

She responded, "Well, I think you're doing a very good job, but..."

"But what?" I said.

"Well, I'm really not used to this new kind of preaching. So son, let me give you some advice. If you are going to make it as a preacher, you're going to have to learn, don t try to teach me anything, just make me feel good."

I laugh about that incident to this day, but there is something in that illustration that carries a sense of hopelessness.

Is the church merely a place we go to feel good? Is it merely a place designed to make us feel better about ourselves? Or is there something else to the church that can take away the lack of hope, faith and courage in a volatile society such as ours?

One day a leader of the early Church had a run-in with hopeless people. During his day, a very young church in a city called Corinth was the watering hole for the Christian elite. The multiple gifts of the Holy Spirit were very evident. Everything was functioning the way it should, or at least the way the Corinthians thought it should. They had prophecies, tongues, healings and mighty miracles. Every spiritual gift you could think of was in the Corinthian church, yet something was wrong. The Corinthian church was having a good time, but they were not maturing in character.

It seems that a certain belief had slipped in the back door of the church. The rumor being whispered was that there was nothing beyond this life—nothing. In other words, there was no resurrection of the dead.

So Paul wrote, "If in this life only we have hope in Christ, we are of all men the most pitiable" (I Cor. 15:19). Now this suggests that there are people whose hope only goes as far as this mortal life. Remember, Paul was writing to a young church. He was not writing to people who did not believe his writings; he was writing to people who agreed with him from the beginning, he was writing to Christians. Paul said in essence that if this life is all we have to look forward to, then we are a bunch of miserable people!

When I first studied this passage, I saw it only as the apostle Paul saying if we don't believe in the life beyond, then we are miserable. But he was saying something much more. In essence, if our hope is limited only to the present realities of this dimension, we are in trouble. If we find the fulfillment of our hopes, dreams, goals and expectations in this world only, then let us weep now—for everything is lost.

I have come face to face with life, face to face with death and face to face even with the life beyond. When Angela passed on (see Chapter 2), I found myself open, hurt, vulnerable, stripped and more sensitive to the things of the Spirit of God than ever before. I do not make any apologies for the fact that I have been affected permanently. At times, I am emotionally drained, but my spirit is energized because my hope extends to the promise of what Jesus has accomplished through the Resurrection.

Now those who have not experienced the passing of a loved one have a tendency to see the Resurrection either as an event to personally anticipate or as a power that keeps us in the present realm of life. This is all true, but to the believers who have watched loved ones go on into the next dimension, the Resurrection carries a special hope. The resurrection is the hope that those who have "fallen asleep" in Christ are not lost and that we who remain on this side will see them again. It is this hope which provides sanity.

Hopeless people are miserable people. We encounter miserable people all the time. They go to church miserable, and unfortunately, they leave the church miserable. Their marriages are miserable, their finances are miserable, their religion is miserable, their outlook is miserable. They're also miserable on their jobs, in their homes and in their relationships.

One day I took the time to really meditate on the question, "If the Church is the Body of Christ on earth and the Body draws its strength from the head, then why is there so much misery among God's people?" The answer is simple. People have no hope for tomorrow because they cannot see beyond today. It is why people wallow in the confusion of things around them. Their misery is an indication that they have no hope beyond this life. Unfortunately, hopelessness leads to depression.

We've all experienced hopelessness at one time or another in life. Even those whom we regard today as highly successful can tell you stories of times when the sun didn't always shine.

Don Meares is one of those. He's a man who faced a challenge and almost lost. Don is the senior pastor of a very influential church in the Washington, D.C., area. Being a pastor is nothing unusual, unless your congregation is 95 percent black. Nothing unusual about that? Well, it is if you happen to be white!

To those who know him, Don Meares is the older brother you never had. His graying hair may suggest stuffiness, that is until he disarms you with his wit and boyish charm. His anecdotes and satire border on sacrilege, yet in the end, you just know God gets a real kick out of this boy!

I asked, "Don, have you ever felt, uh...hopeless?"

There was a space of several seconds. Don propped his feet on the edge of the glass-covered coffee table. He glanced at me and then away. The thought lines on his forehead softened.

"My background is that I was raised in church as a preacher's kid," Don grinned. "At an early age, I felt that I was going to be in the ministry, so I left home and decided that I was going to see what the world was all about. But before that happened, I had an experience that sort of apprehended me. My father, whom I had always looked up to and had always had a great relationship with, asked me if I would become the church's janitor for about a month, because the janitor had just died. I said fine, but that month turned out to be five years! So, here I am, out of college, and I am the white janitor of an all-black church. From my perspective, the man whom I loved and admired, my hero, my father, now had become my employer or my authority in a different sense. He now controlled everything that was important to me, as far as my goals, my income level and my climbing the ladder of success.

"It was funny being the janitor. The people in the church would talk and say, 'Meares, what does he do? You haven't heard? He's got the toilet ministry!' All of that made an impact on me, and I just almost totally, literally lost any hope. It was a completely dead-end situation in which I felt that my whole future was locked. It was fixed. It was determined. Everything I wanted to attain was controlled by my father, and our relationship had totally deteriorated. In his mind, I was lazy, worthless and no good for anything. We had had a great relationship, until I went to work for him. From my perspective, I was being paid way below minimum wage and doing all kinds of things that had nothing to do with the goals I wanted to achieve. So, for the first time in my life, I, being a very cheerful, happy-go-lucky, couldn't-get-me-down sort of person, encountered literally a spirit of depression which was always on me and around me. I think hopelessness and depression go together. They're bedfellows. When you don't have hope of achieving your dreams, ambitions and goals, you get depressed. The two go hand in hand.

"I remember bouts of depression. The first time I ever experienced it was when I would lie in my bed, and I would speak in my mind to God and say, *God, You can't break me, I'm too strong for You. You can't break me.* I would have these bouts of being so depressed, feeling so down and so worthless, then I would have moments of some euphoria like I was an eagle flying high, but it was all unrealistic. I'm not an expert in depression, but these were the symptoms I was going through. It didn't make any sense, because I felt myself being bounced from the ceiling down to the floor in a rapid period of time. I mean within minutes going from an emotional high to a low; there was no stability. All was because of hopelessness. Every dream that was dear to me was gone."

"Were you married?" I asked.

"Yeah."

"During all of these events?"

"Oh, yes! My older brother, well, we both basically started about the same time, same goals. He was immediately elevated as pastor under Dad and was immediately given everything, and I had 'squat'— nothing! That was depressing. Not that I was that much of an incompetent, but, uh...well, it was depressing. I mean, you grow up with your brother, and then you're working with your brother, and you know he's got the income, he's got the car, he's got the salary, he's got platforms, and you've got nothing and you have a family to take care of. It dehumanizes you! You lose your dignity!"

"What happened then?"

"After five years of being a janitor, I went into construction, again with our church. They basically put me in the same position; I was just cleaning the toilets in the construction site. It was there that I began to come out of depression, because I could achieve some goals. That was what eventually brought me out, even though the goals weren't the goals that I had for my life."

"Now, what exactly brought you out?"

"Like I said, when I got into construction. Even though I started as the person who cleaned the toilets, I had another boss, and I felt, well, if I could achieve certain things, I could write my own ticket, and I did. Within a couple of months, I was put on the Sheetrock™ crew with the men who owned the company. Within a few more months, I rose to foreman of his crew, which was unheard of. I just excelled! I was never mechanical until that time. It was just an opportunity to get out of where I was, and I began to see some light of achievement. I was motivated, because being depressed is absolutely no fun. Just making a salary that brought some dignity to my home situation made a difference. We were living out of a one-bedroom apartment. We had one kid, another one was coming, and we didn't have any room. Even though construction was not my goal, as far as what I was supposed to do with my life, it was at least an exit from what I felt was a totally fixed, determined and hopeless situation.

"I remember when the Sheetrock™ and ceiling part was over for that job. My whole fear was, well, what do I do now? Do they put me back to being janitor of the construction site and cleaning toilets? Do they put me back in the church as a janitor? What's going to happen to me? That fear was calmed when I went to other higher phases in construction and ended up being second-in-command on the job site. I was ordering all of the supplies and working with the subcontractor. So, I mean, I just kept rising higher.

"Then, of course, the fear resurfaced to some small degree! Now that the job site is complete, what am I going to do? The good thing was that, in my Dad's eyes, I had grown to a place of accountability and responsibility. When the job site was complete, I hadn't achieved any of the goals that I had for my life, but at least now I was in church administration. You know, where you can take over the printing of the church? You can 'sell' that, and you can do more? At least I could keep achieving, and I did.

I went from construction to dealing with the ministry of the church, which finally got me to where I wanted to be. They would say, 'Well, we'll let you teach a class.' That was my perspective, and those things kept accelerating over what I considered to be a long period of time, something like 13 years, until I finally got to the place that now I was travelling and ministering in churches.

"All of these things happened, and I learned my lesson in one dose. The first five years were when I touched, for the first time in my life, just hopelessness and depression."

Don's face remained motionless, there was no expression. I searched for a smile, a twitch or a frown, but there was none. He was just recalling things he had chosen to pack away. There was no pain or bitterness in his voice, just the tone of a man who had settled some things a long time ago.

"You're now senior pastor," I said. "You travel and speak across the country. Most people would consider that to be very successful. You've built a new church facility. What is the project worth, about six million dollars?"

Don quickly corrected me, "About 12 million dollars!"

Don smiled, but it wasn't a smile of arrogant accomplishment. It was a smile of recollection, knowing that somehow this project was a miracle from God.

"Of course, the church is growing and expanding." I asked. "How much time was it, between the janitor job and now?"

"I think 18 years."

"Eighteen years?"

Don took a deep breath and, while releasing it, said, "Yes, 18 long years."

"Well, at least you're in good company," I said. "I think it took the apostle Paul 17 years from his first calling."

Don smiled, "How about that?"

What is it that enables powerful men and women to forge ahead in spite of circumstances? *The ability to see.*

In Psalms we read, "I will lift up my eyes to the hills; from whence comes my help?" (Ps. 121:1, Moffat's translation) The original Hebrew indicates a special pause marked by a semicolon after the word *hills.* This tells us that there is more to see than meets the eye. It reads, "I will lift up mine eyes unto the hills; From whence cometh my help?" The second verse then answers the question, "My help comes from the Lord, who made Heaven and earth."

It seems that when travelers journeyed through valleys, they would encounter hills loaded with shrines to pagan gods. The psalmist probably was gazing one day at a horizon dotted with pagan altars and temples and said, "I will lift up my eyes unto the hills...," but as he saw the hills filled with lifeless shrines to lifeless gods, he questioned, "Where does my help come from?" Does it come from these monuments on the hills? Of course not! "My help comes from the Lord, who made Heaven and earth," or the God who sits above the hills these false gods sit upon. The psalmist saw a Kingdom that was beyond the gods and the kingdoms of this life. This gave him hope.

In the Gospel of John, Jesus answers Pilate with a reference to another Kingdom. He said, "My kingdom is not of this world. If My kingdom were of this world, My servants would fight..." (John 18:36). Notice that He said, "My servants would fight...." " Jesus alludes to another realm beyond this one that is filled with servants and forces. This expresses hope.

At another time, a man named Abram was childless. As the story goes, God told him to gaze upon the stars. He told Abram that the stars he saw represented the sea of mankind destined to come from his being. God also told him that his name would no longer be Abram but Abraham, "...for I have made you a father of many nations" (Gen. 17:5). Of course, Abraham's initial view was stars, but gradually the hope within Abraham enabled him to see beyond the natural celestial bodies and to perceive a nation, the faces of the future redeemed. This gave him hope.

God told another man by the name of Joshua, "See! I have given Jericho into your hand..." (Josh. 6:2). Joshua was able to see the walls of Jericho fall down before it actually happened. He was able to see God's view, in spite of natural circumstances. Joshua had hope.

In the Bible, there is a passage we call the hall of faith (see Hebrews 11). It's a chapter about people who were able to see into an invisible dimension. It paints the portrait of ordinary people of faith who saw beyond famines, economic crashes, plagues and even death; and yet regardless of the outcome, believed in something beyond. They knew there was hope.

These and other instances give a very vivid outline of how to avoid hopelessness. Hopeless people see only the hopelessness of society. Their hopelessness breeds misery, and miserable people are people who cannot see the reign of Christ in this present world. Unlike our examples, hopeless people will always be miserable people.

People who emphasize hope only in this dimension seldom see any real value in answers from the Kingdom of God. Think about it. We live in a society with a commodities mentality. We call a broker, buy stocks and bonds, and then believe life is a little more secure. We even try to involve God by praying, "God, I really need a new Mercedes." Next we pray, "Now, Lord, it's time to move into a bigger house," or, "Lord, it's time to upgrade my career." Americans have a commodities mentality, so it is no wonder that when we go to church the attitudes remain the same. Not only that, but we frequent the places that teach us how to acquire more commodities! We soon start to believe that if we just pray to God or call up our "spiritual financial advisor," He'll give us whatever we want. We begin to believe that if we give God a certain amount of money, then God will give us a certain amount of money back in order to pay our bills. When it comes to salvation, do we want Christ in our lives for who He is, or do we want Him as just another commodity?

It stands to reason that if our hope is in this dimension only, we will not seek the answers we need from God's point of view. We do not invest in what we don't believe. Where there is no hope, there are questions without answers. Even if God Himself appeared from the sky, saying, "Be thou all knowing...," most people would explain it away as merely a gimmick of a TV evangelist or special effects straight from a Steven Spielberg movie.

The Kingdom of God is always visible to those who seek a hope beyond natural dimensions. God is calling a new generation to view things from a supernatural standpoint. He's calling us to view certain beliefs as sacred once again.

The death, burial and resurrection of Jesus Christ was the plan of God, so we will be able to see the Father's plan when we set our eyes beyond the circumstances of this dimension and realize that satan does not run the show!

I once received a prayer request from a woman battling a terminal disease. She was more worried about her husband than herself. Her husband had told her that if she died, he would never be able to believe in God again. This man's hope and faith were limited to physical death, a passing event in time.

When we understand that God is greater than death, hope explodes within us. Death was not the end of Jesus, and death is not the end of those who trust His Word. As Christ lives, we live also. His resurrection is the hinge upon which our hope swings. When adversity comes, the Bible reminds us, "For He must reign till..." (I Cor. 15:25). When we're able to understand God's purpose, God's plan and God's timing, even beyond adversity, then we can begin to experience the realm Jesus was seeing when He said satan had nothing in Him (see John 14:30).

People often say, "The devil is always picking on me!" "He's on my track!" "The devil stole my money (my wife, my husband, my car)!" These are miserable people who don't know what to do or how to live. But why are they miserable? Because they have no hope. They have no hope because they cannot see the present reign of Jesus

Christ or His Kingdom. They cannot see the invisible beyond the visible. They cannot see the eternal beyond the temporal.

Hope springs from the Resurrection, and resurrection hope is more than the belief that we live on after the physical body dies.

Recently, I had the opportunity to go skiing for the first time, a very interesting experience. I had learned to ski on one of those moving carpet machines in a sporting goods store! Learning the basics on a carpet machine is not the same as skiing on snow, believe me! When I finally got to the ski resort, I decided rather than go to the beginners' class, I would upgrade about two levels. After all, I was a "carpet skiing expert!" I received a rude awakening! I realized, after I had become the focus of a convergence of 12 ski instructors, tumbled down a very large hill several times, and finally was escorted to the "bunny" hill, that I had not learned my lessons very well. It would be safe to say that at that point I was a little nervous about skiing.

I regained my confidence after going through the "new skiers class." But while going up the mountain on a chairlift, my eyes caught small children skiing very smoothly down the mountain. These children were about five or six years old, and I could not believe what I saw. They were skiing effortlessly! They were falling, standing, falling, standing, falling and standing again. It didn't seem to bother them. They laughed with each fall and continued to grin from ear to ear as they mastered their turns. I could not believe that these children had learned so fast. I asked the ski instructor, "How long have they been taking lessons?" "Oh, about a day, or a day and a half," he replied. My eyes got big as saucers! I could not believe it. I asked, "How is it possible for these children to learn so fast, while so many adults (like me) seem to take so long just learning how to get down the bunny hill?" The ski instructor replied, "Because they believe the words of the instructor and expect those words to work."

This is the essence of releasing hope. Unfortunately, as adults we are bombarded by many circumstances, situations, media reports, newspapers and magazine scandals. We could almost suffocate in this atmosphere of hopelessness. Yet, if we are to regain the ability to expect, dream and envision, we must learn to trust the words of the Instructor. This literally means taking God at His Word as a child would. I believe Jesus referred to this when He said, "Allow children to come to me, for the Kingdom of God is made up of the attitude of children" (my paraphrase of Mark 10:14). When we take steps to expect again, it is at that time we will begin to see the physical manifestation of our dreams.

There are several things that I believe are very necessary to releasing the hope that is in you. We read in the Bible a very unique phrase that says, "...Christ in you, the hope of glory" (Col. 1:27). Notice that it does not say, "Christ in you, the glory," but "Christ in you, the hope of glory." This phrase is one of potential. It is the dream of something not yet realized. Hope is a seed within you. *Christ in you is hope, ready and waiting to be released.* Hope is ready to be unleashed upon the things that are around you; it is ready to go, ready to develop and ready to explode. If we can get past the hindrances to our expectations, then that tiny seed of hope will grow until it not only changes things within, but also things in our outward spheres of influence.

Go beyond your past experiences. In other words, leave the past in the past! Your past will color your present and dictate your future. How many people do you know who were abused by a parent or molested by an adult during their childhood and still find themselves carrying that baggage in their present adult life? There are those who have experienced marital failure which led to a traumatic divorce. They thought the pain was over, but when the next man or woman came along, they realized they had carried the previous relationship into the new one. Your past has an effect on the future. Because of previous divorces, there are those who expect nothing from marriage. Because of a previous low-paying job, many people expect nothing or at least very little from another career. But we must learn to erase the past. The apostle Paul said, "...but one thing I do, forgetting those things which are behind and reaching forward to those things which are ahead..." (Phil. 3:13).

Inside you there are two elements: the potential greatness and "the weeds." These two entities war against one another. If we can tap the power of the hope within us, then the weeds of the past and ghosts of yesterday will not choke nor haunt our future. We have the ability to unhook ourselves from the effects of the past as an engine unhooks from a box car. Take the time to realize that you do not have to be commandeered by your yesterdays. When Christ invades us, He erases the scars of yesterday and gives us a new outlook, new expectations, new dreams and new goals.

Go beyond your religion. Whenever you reach the point of hopelessness, consider that the problem may be how you view Christianity or biblical concepts. In

Christ, there is never a lack of hope. In some teaching circles we are told, "There is no way out of your circumstances, so just take life as it comes." In the natural sphere, this philosophy may be right. But in Christ there is always a way out!

For example, it's very interesting how some people can be so strongly opinionated when it comes to whether God still heals today. We may wax theologically eloquent on either aspect of that doctrine, but if we get sick and want to live, then we realize the issue is not doctrine, not denomination and not theology. We find the issue is a need, the need to live. When something hurts, we will find ourselves hungry for any word from God that will give us the hope or expectation of getting well.

We are confronted daily with people who are experiencing abject poverty. It's one thing to give up a great fortune in order to follow Jesus, but it is another thing to tell those who have never had a great fortune to "give it up." At least let them experience what it means to have something, in order to make the contrast!

Being poor is somehow presented as a portrait of holiness. When a person grows up not having financial advantages, it's not good enough to teach them there is something holy about poverty. Poor people want a word from God that will get them out of their poverty. They want the hope that they can get a good education and find a better job. They want to know it's possible to feed their families well or possible to take a vacation every now and then. We must move past our pious and religious viewpoints.

Go beyond your present view of Christ. Jesus is constantly saying to us that He is more than a Provider, more than a Prophet, more than a Water-walker, more than a Messiah and more than a Healer. He tells us that He is the Resurrection and the Life, and not just the Life, but our life. Jesus is more to us than we commonly think of Him.

When the name of Jesus Christ is mentioned, most people think about a poor carpenter who walked around with a sour look on His face doing good deeds. But that's not Jesus. During His time on earth, Jesus was strong, robust and a man of conviction and great assurance. When we find ourselves in great need of comfort, healing, victory, deliverance and providence, we need more than just a common, weak, foggy-thinking carpenter. We need a Jesus who knows who He is, knows from where He has come and knows where He's going.

Regardless of what has happened in the past and regardless of our religious views, if we are to hope again, we must take the limits off Christ in our thinking, and as we change our views, we will change our actions.

Every morning when you get up or every night before you go to bed, stand in front of the mirror, point a finger at the person you see and say,

1. I expect the best each morning.

2. I expect a miracle today.

3. I expect God to keep His Word.

Hope gives form to your faith. Jesus had the hope of feeding multitudes of people when He blessed two fish and five loaves of bread. Three Hebrew boys had a hope of deliverance which empowered them to fearlessly enter a fiery furnace. It was the hope of vindication that enabled Daniel to sleep comfortably in a lion's den; it was the hope of victory that enabled a boy named David to stand toe to toe with a giant while carrying only a sling shot and a stone; and it was the hope of resurrection that enabled Jesus to go meekly, yet with assurance, to the cross of Calvary. Therefore, it will be the same hope, expectation, dream and vision that will enable you to get through the traumas and tragedies of everyday life.

Faith is the substance of things hoped for, but before faith can be activated, it must have a form in which to work. What hopes lie hidden in the nooks and crannies of our minds? What dreams of unwritten books, untitled songs or untried inventions have failed to explode upon society because of our unbelief? What visions have remained visible to us and us alone? Well, hundreds, probably thousands.

Hopes that remain unreleased are like buried treasure—valuable but useless. The Bible refers to hope as a living thing (see I Pet. 1:3), and living things must be fed. So feed your hope the Word of God. Tell it that "all things are possible." Tell it, "I can do all things through Christ who strengthens me" (Phil. 4:13). Talk to your hope today and talk to it again tomorrow. Feed it with words of faith until it begs to be born. Then as a woman in labor, push with all your might and give it all you've got. For the world is waiting to see your newborn dream.

> *Dear God, I stir up the hope that is within me. I now release it into the world to work on my behalf. I activate the hope that You have placed within, and I see myself in Your eternal plan and purpose. As long as You live in me, I can never accept hopelessness again. Amen.*

10

Purpose— A Reason for Going On

Jesus knowing that the Father had given all things into His hands, and that He was come from God, and went to God; He riseth....

John 13:3-4 (KJV)

You can either quit right here or go back and kick the devil's butt." These words were my constant driving companion for over 1,400 miles due east from the West Coast (see Chapter 2). "You've been through the fire, my son, now you are ready for ministry." These words from an elder statesman of the ministry reminded me of who I was when I did not feel much like who I was.

For each and every one of us there is a reason for being on this planet. Although we hear this constantly, we still have the tendency to lose our sense of destiny every now and then. I don't know, maybe it comes from religious backgrounds through which we were taught to deny ourselves or consider ourselves lower than the lowest worm. Maybe it's those songs we sing which drum up images of worthlessness. Or maybe it's the fear of feeling our own oats! Could it be religion's way of keeping us chained to legalistic creeds, fearing that we might be released upon the world and somehow forget our Creator? Well, I don't believe God fears that His creation will run very far away from Him. I can't imagine God falling off His throne and throwing a temper tantrum each time some human doesn't believe. God is too assured of Himself. He knows that the entire earth will be filled with His glory, whether one generation accepts their destiny or not.

God sees everything, from the beginning straight to the end. He knows the outcome. After all, He's the greatest strategist ever to live. He knows that when we get beside ourselves life has a way of bringing us full circle to the question, "Where is God?"

God made us in His image, but through no fault of His, we chose to exchange that image in order to "find" ourselves. God knows that without Him we merely wander in circles, so He waits, knowing that sooner or later, somewhere down the road, we will come face to face with ourselves, only to be reminded that we were not created in our own image.

The same questions keep popping up. Is there an intelligence, a power, a force behind everything in the universe? Could it be that every star we gaze upon has been gazed upon long before we were born? Are we to conclude that we are merely simple creatures that exploded upon this planet for no apparent reason? I don't think so.

As men and women we think, we dream, we plan, we have hopes, and we consider the coming generations in our preparation for the future. We are more than evolved slime; we were placed upon this planet to perpetuate some type of plan. Yes, there is a reason we are here. If we were to use another word to express this, it would be the word *purpose*.

Purpose is the driving force of man. It's what keeps us intact. Purpose wakes us when the alarm clock buzzes in the morning. It's what assures us when we leave our homes for work that there is a reason for us to be there. After a stressful day we race home, knowing there is a purpose for our families. We eat knowing there is a purpose for food and sleep knowing that there is even a purpose for those hours of solitude. The truth of the matter is that you can exist, but you cannot truly live without purpose.

Take an automobile, for example. Purpose may not supply the knowledge of how it functions, but purpose is why you buy it. Purpose is what helps us to distinguish which course of action to take in our everyday routines. It is what goes before us, calling us to go beyond present reality, while with each step, assuring us of why we're doing it in the first place.

Webster's Dictionary defines purpose as "to aim, to intend, to resolve or plan." Purpose is not the clothing, but the pattern from which a garment is made.

Often people speak of losing purpose. But purpose is never lost, it is just hiding smugly beneath the rubble of our hurts, fears, pains and disappointments. Unfortunately, many have lived without purpose for so long that they soon learn to live without it at all.

Since God does not waste energy, it stands to reason you were created for a purpose. As a matter of fact, you are the purpose of God made flesh. When you were born, your purpose was resident in you in seed form. The goal is for the seed to germinate and grow into a visible form.

The Bible says, "...the Word became flesh and dwelt among us, and we beheld..." (John 1:14). Notice the word *beheld.* To behold something means you have the ability to see it. Ideas and intents cannot be seen unless they somehow can be housed in flesh. Consequently, the ultimate goal of life is to see the seeds of purpose that God planted in you grow and fulfill God's intent for you.

I remember that as a child in elementary school, every spring we were given several packets of seeds. We were told to go home and plant them. This excited me. I could not wait to get home, plant the seeds and see the results. Every seed packet had a picture of what those specific seeds would produce. I especially loved the sunflower seeds, because if I could grow the largest sunflower head, I would win the school contest. So when I planted the seed, in my mind I kept a picture of that sunflower; not only that, but I was instructed to take the seed packet, place a small stick through it and put it in the ground to remind me of what I had planted and where I had planted it. Every morning, I would faithfully go out to see whether my plant had begun to sprout. The picture on the packet assured me that a sunflower was coming out of the ordeal.

Note the following passage from Isaiah 55:10 (AMP):

For as the rain and snow come down from the heavens, and return not there again, but water the earth and make it bring forth and sprout, that it may give seed to the sower and bread to the eater, so shall My word be that goes forth out of My mouth; it shall not return to Me void—without producing any effect, useless—but it shall accomplish that which I please and purpose, and it shall prosper in the thing for which I sent it.

This passage of Scripture captures the essence of how God gets out of you what He puts into you. It's a passage about purpose. Let's dissect it.

What gives seed to the sower and bread to the eater? Well, according to this passage, it is not the rain or the snow. It's the earth that gives bread to the eater and seed to the sower. So bread for eating and seed for sowing is the accomplished purpose of the earth.

If we go back into the "book of beginnings" (Genesis), we find passages of Scripture that talk about creation: "...Let there be light...And God made the beast of the earth...Let the waters under the heavens be gathered...." But there is a passage in Genesis 1:11 that talks about how God created plant life:

Then God said, "Let the earth bring forth grass, the herb that yields seed, and the fruit tree that yields fruit according to its kind, whose seed is in itself, on the earth"; and it was so.

It is here that God says what the earth is capable of or has the potential to do. When God spoke, He spoke to the earth and commanded it to yield something.

Now let's look at Genesis 1:26:

Then God said, "Let Us make man in Our image, according to Our likeness; let them have dominion over the fish of the sea, over the birds of the air, and over the cattle, over all the earth and over every creeping thing that creeps on the earth."

In this passage, we find what man is capable of or has the potential to do. When God made vegetation, He spoke to the earth. When God made man, He spoke to Himself. Just as the potential for fruitfulness (vegetation) is in the earth, the potential for human life is in God. Just as the potential for human life is in God, so the potential for extending God's plan for the universe is in you!

When God made you, He literally put a designated course inside. From the time you were born, God made sure that every single event in life would be connected to the purpose that He planted inside you.

When we read the passage about the earth bringing forth, a lot of people look at it as if to say, "Wow, God just made these things from nothing; apple and orange trees just sprang up out of the earth." Was it magic? A miracle? Was God creating something for the first time? Well, not really. So, why did the earth produce? Easy, there was seed in it!

According to the King James Version, Genesis 1:28 reads "...replenish the earth...." "Re-" means "to do again." In order to replenish something, there has to have been something there before. From this passage we gather that when God spoke to the earth, He spoke to something that was in the earth. What was there? Seeds! Plain ordinary seeds! From this we can understand that there must also be something placed in us by God. What's in us are seeds of purpose. Although they're in us, getting the results out of us is another story.

So how does God get purpose flowing out of us? The same way he got vegetation out of the earth. Just as God spoke to the earth to make the vegetation appear, so He speaks to us to cause the purposes placed within us to appear. What have we learned so far?

1. It's not the rain or snow that gives bread to the eater and seed to the sower, it's the earth.

2. Rain and snow symbolize the Word of God.

3. It is not the Word that brings forth here, but that on which the Word rains.

4. As the rain is the catalyst (or energizer) of what's in the earth, so the Word of God is the catalyst (or energizer) of what's in the human spirit.

There are seeds within the human spirit. Not just one or two, but conglomerations or pockets of various kinds. These seeds are the purposes of God. If the Word of God is allowed to rain upon them, they will ultimately germinate and produce whatever they have been programed to produce.

Notice I used the word *programed*. While doing some study in the field of biology, I ran across something called DNA or the "molecular structure of a living thing." DNA is the biological program that determines what we are and how we function.

The early Greeks believed that "seeds, plants or animals must already contain within them the form, nature or essence of the species from which they came." They believed from the very beginning that if the female of a species, say a cat, became impregnated, the fetus was already designed to be a cat. Therefore, the goal of the genetic code would be to become "as much cat" as possible. They concluded the same for human beings. It's very interesting how medical science has a tendency to draw from the early Greeks, rather than go all the way back to Genesis where God said, "...seed according to its kind...."

As human beings, we were created after our own kind, which is God. We were created with the ability to:

1. Have dominion—rule things that could be ruled.

2. Subdue—rule things that defy ruling.

3. Transcend—move from one level of existence to another.

4. Reproduce—produce after our own kind that which was first produced by God.

Just as we have DNA, we also have "SDP, Spiritual Destiny Program." Man was destined to act like God. He was created to reach up and to reach out. But man turned inward and began to probe and reach within himself. Without God, he found selfishness, envy, division, jealousy and self-deification. His program was all messed up.

This is where the message of the gospel emerges with great clarity. Jesus Christ came in the flesh in order to reprogram man's SDP (Spiritual Destiny Program). Christ came to enable man to reach up and out again.

Let me give you an illustration. When you go to college, you are actually planting inside yourself seeds of knowledge concerning a specific subject. One day you will graduate from college (or some type of training) and reap the harvest of a career.

When you marry, you are planting and exchanging seeds of information about yourself. You are planting seeds of intimacy and seeds of past generations into the other spouse's life. As your marriage progresses, you should eventually reap a harvest of relationship, children and future generations.

When you become part of a local church, you plant seeds of relatiohship, time and even money into the purpose of that church. Out of that local church, you will reap the harvest of expanding God's purposes in the earth. By doing this you ensure a better planet and a better life for you and your children.

These seeds of purpose will remain dormant in our lives until a demand is placed upon them. You can sit around with a lot of collegiate knowledge, but it will never do you any good until that specific job or career demands that you put your knowledge to work. You can have a beautiful wedding, with rows of bridesmaids and groomsmen, and eventually acquire a house with a white picket fence, 2.3 children and a two-car garage. But it is the difficult times, the misunderstandings, and the times that you must stretch in order to make the marriage work that will prove whether that marriage will continue. It's the demands that are placed upon the marriage that draw those seeds of purpose out.

This is why the Bible says, "...in everything give thanks....." Of course, we are not thankful for bad things, tragedies or pressures. No way! I, like you, would love to avoid them all! Yet God is able to use these demands in order to draw from us what has been placed within us from the beginning. What has been placed within us is the power and potential to overcome anything.

It is when we find our place and purpose in life that we begin to realize the problems, challenges and tragedies surrounding us are really insignificant. We discover that the most important thing in life is to discover what is the most important thing in life.

It's the same in everyday life. As long as you know there is a higher purpose, the transitory things, the hurts, deaths, pains and sicknesses don't bother you as much, because you know you can rise above them.

My kingdom is not of this world. If My kingdom were of this world, My servants would fight...but now My kingdom is not from here.... For this cause I was born, and for this cause I have come into the world...Jesus, knowing that the Father had given all things into His hands, and that He had come from God and was going to God.... (John 18:36,37; 13:3)

For we know that if our earthly house of this tabernacle were dissolved, we have a building of God, an house not made with hands, eternal in the heavens. (II Cor. 5:1, KJV)

Jesus Christ and the apostle Paul, among others, are people who knew how to "live on the top." Nothing can hurt you on the top. This is where God has always intended for us to live. He has uttered words like, "I will make you the head and not the tail;" the above only and not the beneat (see Deut. 28:13).

Going on in spite of circumstances always depends upon a reason. Someone once said that you can live several days without food or water, but you cannot live one second without hope. Whenever you talk to someone who is contemplating suicide, they are weighing whether their life has purpose or not. The moment they come to the conclusion that their life is meaningless is the moment they die.

Some may call the concept of "living on the top" mental escapism. I call it living as God lives. God does not go through trauma or fall off His throne because of earthly mishaps. Why? Because God sees the outcome. He knows what's around the corner. He knows that somehow you will overcome the situation! Of course, He's disappointed if you do not take your options; but even if you do not take your options, God has other options to compensate for the options you missed!

So tell me, what could possibly be a reason for going on? Your existence is proof of your worth. You were not haphazardly born to haphazardly take up space. You have a mind, a personality, a will and a desire to rise and fly above your present state.

"Before I formed thee in the belly I knew thee; and before thou camest forth out of the womb I sanctified thee...." (Jer. 1:5, KJV). When God talks about knowing you, He is not talking about the name given to you by your parents. Webster's Dictionary defines the word *name* as "a word or words expressing some quality considered characteristic or descriptive of a person or thing; reputation or character...." A name is parallel with character, so before you were born, God was intimate with your character, your personality, your intellect and your potential in life.

"...I am fearfully and wonderfully made..." (Ps. 139:14). You were made with an idea in mind. Your worth is evidence of your purpose.

Now hold on to your seats, I am going to get real deep now. Ready? Here goes! If a person goes through school in order to acquire an M.D. degree, specializing in brain surgery, what do you suppose he will become? A brain surgeon, of course! Now that's deep! Silly you say? Not as silly as some people whose gifts are exceptionally evident, yet they cannot figure out what they're supposed to do or be.

God is not going to come out of the sky with a thunderous voice saying, "I command you to be a cab driver." If you can drive a car, if you like people and are disciplined enough to handle your own affairs, then God will allow you the freedom to drive a cab or do whatever else you want to do in that area of talent. That's just the way God works.

For you not to fulfill your purpose is a life wasted. When you finish eating, if something is left on your plate that serves no purpose, what do you do with it? You throw it into the garbage. I believe hell is more than just a place of fire and torment. Hell is the garbage heap of wasted lives. What insect hangs around garbage? Flies, of course. Did you know that one of satan's names is *beelzebub*? Beelzebub is translated "lord of the flies." When a person does not find his or her Creator and the purpose that the Creater has placed in them, then there is nothing else for God to do with that life but allow it to wind up on the garbage heap with the flies!

To connect with God is to connect with your planned purpose. This is why eternal life begins the moment you connect with Christ. Eternal life begins on earth, not in

Heaven. If connection with God grants immediate life, then to remain disconnected from Him dooms us to death. Without God there are but two things left to do—close your eyes and lie down.

There is so much that God wants to do through you. There are other lives besides yours that must experience Him. You are His channel; He desires to love through you, inspire through you, redeem through you and heal through you. He wants to do battle with evil through you, rebuild wasted places through you and reclaim His mighty creation through you. God lives to enable you to liberate people held captive by their own selfishness. His goal is to advance His Kingdom through you.

So, how does this happen? It happens when you write books, preach, teach, educate, get involved and relate to others. It happens when you choose to live and not die. After all, without you, this planet would just not be the same.

11

Chosen to Live

For He chose us in Him before the creation of the world....

Ephesians 1:4 (NIV)

Long before time, there was God. He was in the beginning before planets, galaxies, black holes and nebula. He reigned as light, a pulsating energy, this personality without comparison. The words of an old Negro spiritual sum it up, "He's God all by Himself, He don't need nobody else."

He didn't need anyone else, yet He chose someone else. As a fetus resides warm and safe in the mother's womb, so it was with God's chosen—we were safe in the womb of the Creator before creation began.

How marvelous to know that each personality, each idiosyncracy, each joy, pain, desire and imagination has always been known by God. We were in Him, "...in Him we live and move and have our being..." (Acts 17:28). We began in Him as a seed, a thought ready to be spoken, an experience so fantastic that it could only be called spirit.

We are awed by the miracle of conception, the growth of the fetus in the mother's womb and the ultimate breaking of the water, the pushing, the aggressive force of life emerging from the safety of the mother's care. We are fascinated with the final violent push, forcing a new life into another dimension. We call this birth. As it is in the natural, so it is in the spiritual. God carried us inside Himself, knowing all along that somewhere in time He would speak our name and the violent push of His word would release our new life upon the world. However, with this knowledge comes responsibility.

I imagine the apostle Paul felt it, the inner knowing that he had been chosen to be more than what he presently was. Let's review the Scriptures.

Paul had been accused of insurrection and inciting a riot. Consequently, he was detained by Roman guards. From that point, he was carried before magistrates and other judicial officials to determine the extent of his crime. In each of these courtrooms Paul was able to give a witness to his experience with the Messiah, the Christ. But rather than receive the verdict based on Jewish law, Paul used his right as a Roman citizen to appeal to Caesar. Therefore, he went bound on a course toward Rome.

Paul was under heavy guard on a ship in the middle of a storm. The water was about 120 feet deep, and there was danger of crashing into the rocks nearby. It was night. The sky was cloudy, leaving little ability to navigate. Some of the men had decided to jump ship, but Paul ultimately took unofficial command and persuaded them to stay in the boat, telling them that unless they did, they would not be saved. Finally, when daylight came they searched frantically for a familiar landmark, but much to their dismay, they couldn't recognize the land. They soon noticed a sandy beach not far from their position and decided to run the ship safely aground. They cut loose the anchors and left them in the sea, untied the ropes, hoisted the sail to the wind and tried to make it to the beach. Unfortunately, the ship struck a sandbar with a force so violent that the stern broke into pieces. The crew judged the situation as hopeless and made plans to kill all prisoners to keep them from escaping. But one of the centurions argued to spare Paul's life and kept the others from carrying out their plans. Later the order came for everyone to jump ship and get to land the best way they could.

Until now, the hope of Paul arriving safely in Rome had been very high. But the storm had created doubts, and storms were not to be easily dismissed.

We learn from Paul's experience that everybody, even Christians, will encounter storms. The Bible says it rains on the just as well as on the unjust. Paul writes in an earlier letter,

> *No temptation* [pressure] *has seized you except what is common to man. And God is faithful; He will not let you be tempted beyond what you can bear. But when you are tempted* [pressured], *He will also provide a way out so that you can stand up under it.* (I Cor. 10:13, NIV)

Every human life will experience storms. We don't like it, but it's a fact.

I live near the Gulf Coast, and everyone who lives in this area is conscious of possible hurricanes. The weather service even has a sophisticated way of tracking them. When the announcement of an approaching hurricane is made, people mob the stores, buying bottled water, flashlight batteries and masking tape. The merchants love it! What makes a hurricane so dangerous? Well, it's not the wind. Wind is common. The same force that produces a wind that can level an entire city also produces a summer breeze. The problem is not the wind, it's the speed of the wind. Webster's Dictionary defines storm as "to whirl, move or turn quickly...; in meteorology any wind ranging in speed from 64 to 72 miles per hour constitutes a storm."

A storm is an agitation of wind. Think of agitation in terms of your washing machine. When you turn it on, the action will churn your clothes in water, and with detergent, the dirt will be released from the fabric. The constantly changing direction of a washing machine agitator disrupts the flow of water, and the constantly changing direction of wind causes a storm. This is why we call the agitation of isolated events in our lives storms.

Throughout the New Testament, storms usually preceded some miraculous or significant event. Jesus and His disciples were plagued several times by storms. Yet afterward some of the greatest miracles took place. In one instance, Jesus cast out a legion of devils (Mark 4:35-5:13); in another, the storm was the setting for one of the greatest miracles in the Bible, Peter walking on the water (Matt. 14:28-29). It was also during a storm that Jesus was awakened on a boat trip by terrified disciples; they feared dying in the storm (Matt 8:26). Jesus got up, rebuked them first for having a lack of faith and then rebuked the storm so He could get some sleep! The storm didn't bother Him, but maybe if He stopped the storm, the disciples would shut up!

It often seems that some hidden personality is dedicated to keeping us from experiencing the miracles after the storm. It seems as though satan himself uses the storm in order to keep us from experiencing the blessings and victories that are just on the other side. But tell me, is it possible that we would react more confidently in the storm if only we knew what victories to expect on the other side of it? Probably so.

I'll be the first to admit that it is hard to concentrate on miracles when you're in the storm. Why? Because storms confuse us. We lose our bearings; we lose our sense of direction. Storms seemingly take the control out of our hands, leaving us to battle without defense the natural forces swirling around us.

I can't quite remember where I read it, but there was an article that discussed the mental state of young people who are involved in drug trafficking and gangs. It said that the ideal ones to recruit are teens between the ages of 12 and 16. The reason? They don't fear dying. Teens have not yet developed a full psychological understanding of death. We can go back to our own childhood to recollect this euphoric sense of invincibility. But as we aged, we changed. It was not until adversity had successfully twisted our arms over a period of time that we began to fear, to be cautious, to realize that at any moment we could lose the very thing that was precious to us, our lives.

From a natural point of view, I believe this is what Paul experienced. But there was more to Paul than being a natural man faced with natural fears. He said that it did not matter to him whether he lived or died. For him to live was Christ and to die was gain (Phil. 1:2). What gave him this sense of security? The Scripture reads, "Last night an angel of the God whose I am and whom I serve stood beside me and said, 'Do not be afraid, Paul. You must stand trial before Caesar; and God has graciously given you the lives of all who sail with you'" (Acts 27:23-24 NIV). Notice the phrase *you must. Must* is a powerful word. It carries a sense of compulsion, obligation, require-ment or necessity. During another pressure situation, in Acts 23:11 (NIV), Jesus spoke to Paul telling him to "Take courage! As you have testified about Me in Jerusalem, so you must also testify in Rome." The word *must* is spoken again. This word also hints at destiny. We're beginning to see that the "must" in Paul's life stemmed from a state-ment made to him during his encounter with the "voice in the light."

The apostle Paul at one time in his life had violently opposed the "people of the way," Christians. His opposi-tion was so strong that he sought permission from the religious leaders of his time to act as a vigilante, hunting Christians down, casting them into prison and ultimately sending them to their death. But on one of these journeys, Paul (Saul was his name at the time) was on his way to the city of Damascus when suddenly he saw a light flash before his eyes. He fell to the ground and heard a voice saying, "Saul, Saul, why are you persecuting Me?" Of course, he asked, "Who are You?" The voice said, "I am Jesus, whom you are persecuting" (Acts 9:4-5). This is a key passage because it tells us the reason Paul thought and acted as he did. I've often wondered why Paul would put so much stock in something which could have been merely a dream, a vision or a common upset stomach. Was he hallucinating? What made this encounter pivotal?

Paul heard the voice out of "the light." Any Jewish scholar who knew something about the Shekinah light knew that when a voice spoke from it, it had to be God Himself. It was this understanding that brought him to Damascus, wherein lived another follower named Ananias. Ananias was not too sure about accepting this Saul of Tarsus. But the Lord gave him an unusual word, He told him, "Go! This man is my *chosen instrument* to carry My name before the Gentiles and their kings and before the people of Israel" (Acts 9:15 NIV, emphasis added). It was the phrase *chosen instrument* that I believe prodded Paul for the rest of his life to seek after the knowledge and heart of the "voice in the light."

Webster's Dictionary defines the word *chosen* as "picked out by preference; selected...." *Vine's Expository Dictionary of New Testament Words* also defines the word as "a picking out." No wonder there was a fearlessness in the life of Paul. No wonder there was a courage that defied the natural laws of reason. Paul had been chosen, and he knew he had been chosen! The very word of our Lord that was spoken to him, the "must" of God, gave Paul the stamina to go on, because he knew he had been chosen for something. He carried a sense of destiny, knowing that he *must* survive in order to fulfill it. (So what we are chosen to be in life will also dictate the events that surround and guide our lives.)

God had a specific plan for Paul. Certain truths had to be revealed to future believers. There was a need to understand the hows and whys of the mind of Christ. Paul was chosen to relate these things. He was chosen to align the heartbeat of man with the heartbeat of God. Therefore, it was a "must" that he live. It was a "must" that he carry on his testimony. It was a "must" that hundreds more would hear the account of his conversion. When we plug into the reason we have been chosen by God, then we, too, will experience the "musts" of God speaking to us, convincing us and comforting us, as did Paul.

Jesus, while traveling with His disciples one day, said to them that He *must* go through Samaria. Now in their time, Jews were not too fond of Samaritans. They would even go so far as to walk many miles out of their way to avoid going through Samaria. But Jesus considered Samaria a "must." Because of that urgency many were saved, and the disciples were taught a valuable lesson concerning the lives of those considered to be unwanted or unloved.

Several years ago, I had the privilege of serving a church deep in a rural area of Texas for three and a half years. I went through the process of struggling. I learned what it meant to depend on God for everything. My board of deacons was made up almost entirely of elderly men. They taught me to lead (through experience!). I learned how to be firm, yet diplomatic, and lost the brashness and impatience of youth. I grew up. That experience took a lot out of me, but the church that I now serve is better because of my experience. I now consider that it was a "must" for me to go through that small rural church experience. If I hadn't, I believe that there would be decisions I could not make today! There would be judgments I would make today that I would regret later.

It is knowing that we have been picked out for something greater than ourselves that gives us a sense of fulfillment and satisfaction. How often we want to give up, yet there is something or someone inside that refuses to fail. In spite of it all, we survive. Is the ability to survive some genetic trait passed down only to a select or elite few? Not really. Is the ability to survive only given to one particular race or culture? Not hardly. Is the ability to survive some special award bestowed on one after some ritual or mystic ordeal? Never! The ability to survive is within every creature, yet not every creature uses it. The potential to overcome is within us all, yet not all "come over."

On the ship, Paul gave those who could swim the command to jump overboard. These types are the daredevils, the risk-takers, the ones who go against the odds, getting an adrenaline pump from cheating death. These are the ones who laugh in the face of adversity and consider danger as the ultimate toy. But what of those who never learned to swim? What of those who still struggle with floating or dog-paddling? What of those who fear the enormous danger of the water? Do they deserve to die in the storm because they have not acquired a certain aquatic technique? Of course not! It is here that we catch a glimpse of the unfailing mercy of God, because some came in "on broken pieces" (Acts 27:44). Some of the crew clung for dear life to whatever pieces of the ship were available. So it is with a shipwrecked life; we must cling and make do with what little we have left.

How often I hear the pronouncements of doom on single parenthood. To say that you or your children won't achieve stability because the other parent is not at home is untrue. You are a parent, and you have something in your hand. Being poor and uneducated is a handicap, of course, and I agree that money and education would certainly take the pressure off certain areas of life. But you still have something to offer. What of those who feel the crunch of second-class citizenship because of their color or race? Do they have a chance? What of the disabled? Are they disabled in spirit? No! These situations and more only mean that you've had to make it on broken pieces. There is nothing wrong with broken pieces, as long as you make good use of them.

What is your situation in life? Is it a broken home? Are you suffering poverty? Have you been stereotyped by another race? Have you experienced a divorce? Do you lack the education or the experience to find a decent job? Is your outlook on life still dark? Well, don't be discouraged. The pieces may be broken, but take confidence, you have something in your hand. There have been many who have had only a little, but the miraculous occurred with the little that they had.

Samson, when faced with a potential defeat at the hands of the Philistines, took in his hands the jawbone of a donkey and won the battle hands down (Judg. 15:15). Moses, when commanded by Yahweh to go into Egypt to tell Pharaoh to let His people go that they may worship, questioned God concerning how the people would view his credibility. God's response was simple. He asked Moses what was in his hand. Moses replied, "A rod" (Exod. 4:2). It was the rod that would ultimately become the instrument of Moses to lead the people of God to deliverance. A woman, upon meeting Jesus to inquire about the healing of her child, was questioned by Jesus as to why He should give the bread that belonged to the Jews to those who were not of the house of Israel. The woman in turn asked that she might receive merely "the crumbs which fall from their Masters' table" (Matt. 15:27). A little boy possessed two fish and five barley loaves, not nearly enough to feed one. But when his little was given into the hands of Jesus, it was reported that five thousand men, besides women and children, were fed from this meager meal (John 6:10-13). It's amazing what you can do with broken pieces. So don't sit and cry over spilled milk; we all spill milk at some time or another. The issue is not what you spilled, but how long it takes to clean it up.

Someone once commented to me that I would have a different outlook on life if I experienced a little more failure. I responded to them that I never fail. Of course, eyebrows raised. Unfortunately, we spell the word *fall*, f-a-i-l. Falling is natural, but failing is another story. Falling is not failing. Failure is the refusal to get up, brush yourself off and try again.

The Scripture tells us that after the storm, all of the crew with the apostle Paul made it safely ashore. The swimmers made it as well as those who came in on broken pieces (Acts 27:41-44). It didn't matter how they got there, what mattered was that they got there alive.

It really doesn't matter what you go through; what matters is that you go through! The psalmist said, "Yea, though I walk through the valley of the shadow of death..." (Ps. 23:4). Paul said it with such grace and splendor when he recorded, "We are hard pressed on every side, but not crushed; perplexed, but not in despair; persecuted, but not abandoned; struck down, but not destroyed..." (II Cor. 4:8-9, NIV). This symphony of winning crescendoed when he wrote, "No, in all these things we are more than conquerors through Him who loved us. For I am convinced that neither death nor life, neither angels nor demons, neither the present nor the future, nor any powers, neither height nor depth, nor anything else in all creation, will be able to separate us from the love of God that is in Christ Jesus our Lord" (Rom. 8:37-39, NIV).

So life, do what you will. Christ has given us an alternate route. "I have told you these things, so that in Me you may have peace. In this world you will have trouble. But take heart! I have overcome the world" (John 16:33, NIV). In this world you will have pressure, but He reminds us that in Him we have peace. The place of safety, victory, calmness and surety is in Him.

Wherever there are people willing to overcome, you will find the "musts" of God as a thin thread running throughout their lives.

I could tell you of a family whose son was fatally struck down by a speeding car. I could tell you of a wife whose children were shot by her husband who later committed suicide, leaving her to face life alone. I could tell you of a husband who lost his job, unsure of how he would feed his family. I could tell you of those stricken with AIDS, embarrassed at the thought of revealing the diagnosis to their families. I could tell you of many who come face to face with the disappointments of life, yet somehow find courage to get through. They made it. Of course, I could tell you of the others. Yes, the others—the ones who tried to make it, but didn't. As much as we would love to do so, we can't help them now. But this book is not about them—it's about you. It's about those of you who still have the spark of life.

Hebrews chapter 11 lists many who walked with God by faith. Verse 39 (NIV) says, "These were all commended for their faith, yet none of them received what had been promised." The list could go on and on, enough to fill volumes of books. Verse 40 gives us encouragement. It says, "God had planned something better for us so that only together with us would they be made perfect [complete]."

Yes, there are broken pieces, hurts and losses in life, but through the grace of God, we can turn them into life preservers. When we look at our lives, we may not see all of the tools necessary for winning, but then God does not need very much to help us win. He needs only a little—a little trust, a little hope and a little faith. Even if these are no greater than a grain of mustard seed, it has been said that mountains will move (Matt 17:20).

There must be a sense of destiny about us. We are not accidents. Our birth was not a happenstance. Regardless of the intent of our mothers and fathers, there was another intent spoken millennia ago out of the mouth of God stating who we were to be. We think we chose Him, but no, no—He has chosen us. He has designed a plan, a purpose, a path that will carry us to some glorious future. In the end, God will win. He will conquer all, and He will remain as the ultimate ruler of the creation that was spoken out of His mouth. He reigns, yet He has declared He will not reign alone. For He has promised that we will reign with Him.

Broken pieces are not the issue, the issue is what we do with them. Will we turn them into stepping stones? Will we use them as tools to build, rather than tools to destroy? Will we become one of those who are applauded for overcoming, or will we join the ranks of those who went down without a fight? Well, I think better of us. I believe that after reading this book, something will have been added to life.

Just as God spoke Adam into existence, somewhere in eternity past He spoke our names, and with the speaking of our names, He also commanded a purpose, a reason for being, a predestined set of "musts." There are certain events that *must* take place. After all, He says, "The steps of a good man are ordered by the Lord..." (Ps. 37:23). Steps are not ordered without reason; there is a destination at which you *must* arrive. He tells us that His Word is a lamp unto our feet and a light unto our path (see Ps. 119:105). The definition of the word, path, is "a track or way worn by footsteps." The Master has already gone before us. He has been the example. He has shown us the way. All we have to do is place our feet in His footsteps, and we will arrive at the place He has prepared for us.

Take courage in the fact that we have been chosen. Of millions of sperm, the one which was to produce us survived. We developed and came forth. We are special. But we are not special because of anything we have done or said. We are special because He chose us.

Your life has been planned. Therefore, do not resist the gentle urgings and nudgings that force you into the direction you must go. It is for your good, it is for your pleasure. God promises us that if anything goes wrong, He'll fix it. "And we know that all things work together for good to those who love God, to those who are the called according to His purpose" (Rom. 8:28).

That's me. That's you.

Notes

p. 1   Schuller, Robert. *Tough Times Never Last But Tough People Do*, Garden Grove, CA, Thomas Nelson, 1983, p.64.

p. 3   Houston Chronicle. Houston, Texas, 1991.

p. 18   Montgomery, Edward L: *Breaking the Spirit of Poverty*, (Shippinsburg PA: Destiny Image Publishers, 1988).

p. 56   Brothers, Joyce, Dr. Channel 2 KPRC-TV, Interview with Ron Stone. Houston, Texas, 1992.

p. 61   Kushner, Harold. *Who Needs God.* Simon & Schuster, New York, New York, 1989, p. 43.

p. 71   Kushner, Harold. *Who Needs God.* Simon & Schuster, New York, New York, 1989, p. 43.

p. 83   Archimedes. *A Place To Stand.* Richmond, Indiana, Harper & Row, 1969, p.13.

p. 99   Locke, John. *The Empiricists.* Garden City, NY, Anchor Book, 1974, pp. 13-21.

p. 115 Hordern, William. From "The Case For A New Reformation Theology." The Westminister Press, 1959, pp. 31-52.

p. 127 Bennette, Charles A. *A Place To Stand.* Richmond, Indiana, Harper & Row, 1969, p. 59.

p. 198 Encyclopedia Britanica "Philosophical Athropology," Volume 25, 1990, 15th Edition, p. 558, Column 2.

p. 201 *Webster's New World Dictionary of the American Language*, World Publishers, n.d.

p. 211 Vine, *W.E. Vines Expository Dictionary of New Testament Words*, Iowa Falls, Iowa, Riverside Book & Bible House p. 361.

Breaking the Spirit of Poverty by **Ed Montgomery.** There is a vast difference between what the world calls prosperity and what Jesus said were the "true riches." You can learn how to see once and for all the draining spirit of poverty go out of your life. TPB-156p. ISBN 0-914903-57-8 Retail $5.95

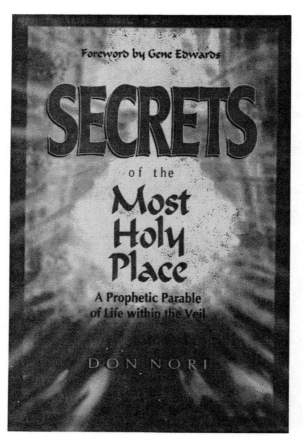

Secrets of the Most Holy Place, by **Don Nori,** is a prophetic parable you will read again and again. The winds of God are blowing. They are drawing you to His Life within the Veil of the Most Holy Place. Secrets long hidden to the casual and passive believer are wonderfully opened. This is not a teaching book or a theological exegesis. It is a living and dynamic experience with God! TPB-182p. ISBN 1-56043-076-1 Retail $7.95